Trials in Heels

K.D. Hunter

 New Generation **Publishing**

CHAPTER ONE

A familiar and unwelcome noise penetrated my dream. I groaned and wished for just a second that I could snuggle deeper into my duvet and ignore it. I rolled over, blindly searching for my phone in the darkness and silently wishing that it wasn't who I expected it would be. The screen told me that it was a 'blocked' number. My heart sank. I held the phone to my ear and took a deep breath of acceptance. 'Hello, Kate Hunter speaking,' I croaked into the phone, trying my best to sound fully alert and professional, but failing miserably.

'Good morning, Miss Hunter. This is Custody Sergeant Fibbs from Battersea Police Station,' a perky and fully awake voice said. 'Are you still dealing with Darrell Clay?'

I hauled myself into a sitting position. 'Yes. Yes I am,' I said sleepily, hoping that my client just wanted to speak to me rather than the alternative.

'The officers are ready for interview.'

Damn. Swinging my legs over the bed, I groped for the light switch, knocking over a glass of water in the process. 'Shit,' I cursed.

'Sorry?' the voice at the other end of the phone asked.

'I mean, I'm on my way. I'll be there within 45 minutes,' I croaked. That would mean I should arrive there at roughly 3.30am. I hung up the phone and not for the first time wondered why I was working in this job. To add to my misery, the book I was reading was now thoroughly soaked with water. Hopefully a few days on the radiator would sort that out.

I shook my head in an attempt to wake myself up and I made an attempt to clean up the water with some tissues while pulling on jeans, boots and a warm jumper. One of the worst things about having to get up in the middle of a winter's night was the biting cold. I prayed the windscreen of the car wouldn't be frosted over.

Creeping down the stairs I tried to avoid the particularly creaky steps in an attempt not to wake my flatmate Laura. She worked as a lawyer in the city and had probably only made it to bed a little while ago. I passed the kitchen and had a quick debate with myself about whether to fill up a travel mug with coffee or not. Making a quick decision, I flicked the switch on the kettle and while I was waiting for it to boil, I shrugged on my coat and wrapped my thickest scarf around my neck. I had a quick look around for my gloves but they were nowhere to be found.

I filled the mug with steaming black coffee, grabbed my bag and headed out the door, bracing myself against the cold. I congratulated myself for bringing the coffee. I shivered as I searched around in my bag for the car keys. God it was *cold.* As I pulled the door of the fiesta shut and turned on the engine, I could see my breath inside the car. Thankfully the windscreen wasn't too badly frosted and a few minutes later the heater had cleared it. At least the traffic will be light at this hour I thought absentmindedly while trying to calculate whether I might get some more sleep before I had to go to court in the morning. Or this morning, I corrected myself.

On arriving at the station, I used the intercom in the reception area to buzz through to the custody suite to announce my arrival. I sat down on a cold blue metal chair, staring around at the empty room. It had the obligatory posters declaring that the Met Police were there to help tackle Crime. Other colourful posters provided phone numbers to call if you were being abused or were a victim of a violent husband.

I sighed and glanced at the clock on the wall. Getting more sleep this morning before court didn't look like it was going to happen. As I sat there, I closed my eyes, shutting out my surroundings.

I hazily heard someone coughing and my eyes snapped open. Unfortunately I was still at the police station. A burly officer was standing in front of me, looking highly amused. My eyes blinked rapidly, assaulted by the harsh lighting.

I stood, trying to pretend that having a snooze at the police station in the middle of the night was the most normal thing in the world.

'Miss Hunter?' he questioned, in a surprisingly feminine voice, for such a hulking man.

I nodded.

'I'm the Officer dealing with the case,' he virtually squeaked. I had to suppress a grin. 'PC Rogers,' he said with a nod. 'Do you want to follow me through to the custody centre?' he asked as he held the door open for me.

As we walked through the snaking corridors, I could hear the noise level rise as we neared the custody reception area. The desk area took up about a third of the room and behind it were about five officers. Two of them were manning the phones and the other two were engrossed in a very lively conversation about yesterday's football.

I walked up to the fifth who I assumed was the Detention Sergeant and waited patiently for a moment or two. When he seemed intent on ignoring me, I coughed and as he raised his head, I shoved my business card in front of him. I was tired. All I wanted to do was get this matter dealt with and I was getting increasingly annoyed with the police for keeping me waiting.

My business card confirmed that I worked for Hardy, Black and Waterman Solicitors. The sergeant scowled at me and handed me Darrell's Custody record. I scanned it for the relevant details, including the arrest time and confirming that he had been arrested for the offence of Robbery. I had known Darrell for the last three years since working for HBW Solicitors. During that time, he had probably spent more time in police custody than he had in school. He was fifteen and one of four children. His mother, Natasha, seemed to have stopped caring about what he got up to years ago. The word was that his father had been shot in a gang retaliation shooting when Darrell had been five. I'm sure psychologists would have a field day with all the issues that probably stemmed from that.

PC Rogers indicated that I should follow him and once again I trailed after him through another set of doors, into an identical set of corridors, lit with florescent lighting. He stopped abruptly and pushed open a door. Inside was a female officer, who I assumed would also be interviewing Darrell. She stepped forward and introduced herself as PC Webster.

The room was the standard interview room. Bare, except for a tape recording machine, a table and four chairs. There wasn't even a rubbish bin as these had been removed after some detained people had become aggressive during interviews and hurled them at the interviewing officers. I sat down and PC Webster handed me typed disclosure, across the table.

This was a summary of the evidence the police had against Darrell. It informed me that he had been arrested at 18.00 yesterday because he matched the description of someone who had robbed an elderly woman. It was alleged that Darrell had approached this woman from behind, pushing her to the floor and grabbing her handbag before making off. I sat back, taking this in and formulating questions to ask officers, in order to get more information from them. I asked if the old lady had provided a description of her attacker but they refused to tell me. I pressed for further information but was met with blank refusals. I took this to mean that the old lady had probably described the attacker as black but as it had been dark and she had been pushed to the ground I assumed that a full and proper description had not be given. My guess, without hearing Darrell's side of the story, was that he was probably found in the vicinity of where the robbery had taken place. He had presumably been arrested because he was so well known to the police and he fitted the description the old lady had provided, in so far as he was black. I asked if Darrell had been found with a handbag or any of its contents on arrest and surprisingly PC Rogers conceded that he had not. I signed the disclosure form, indicating that I didn't have any further questions.

As Darrell was a youth, he would have to be interviewed with an Appropriate Adult present. In Darrell's case this was his older and not so appropriate sister, Kiara. I told the officer that I was ready to speak with my client and both officers disappeared out of the room. A few minutes later a sleepy and dishevelled looking Darrell was bought in to me. Behind him walked Kiara. Despite the early hour, her face was immaculately made up. Her hair was scraped back from her face and gripped in a bun at the back. She wore large gold hoop earrings, tight jeans and a cropped jacket. Obviously doesn't feel the cold, I thought idly to myself.

Cripes, Darrell had really grown since I had seen him about five months ago. He was wearing a baggy red hoody and even baggier jeans. The shoe laces had been taken from his Nike runners which looked brand new. The Detention officers would keep these until he was being released in case he tried to harm himself while in their custody. His shoulders were hunched and he walked like he had the weight of the world on his shoulders.

I gestured to Kiara to take a seat beside me. She flopped into the seat and immediately pulled out her phone.

Darrell brightened on seeing me. 'Alright miss,' was his greeting as he slouched in the chair opposite me. As the officers closed the doors behind them, Darrell started speaking.

'Its all crap innit-just 'cos I'm black. I didn't do nuttin.'

'I know Darrell,' I said aware of the importance of keeping him calm. He had previously become so agitated in an interview that he had tried to grab an interviewing officer by the throat. This had ended in him being charged with assaulting a police officer as well as the matter for which he was being interviewed.

'Darrell, an elderly lady made a complaint of robbery and is describing the attacker as black. Now you and I both know that this isn't enough to link you to the scene. What were you doing around the area where you were arrested yesterday Darrell?'

'Just hangin' miss. I was just waitin' for my girl. I don't know nuttin' about no robbery,' he said in his relaxed, couldn't be bothered South London drawl.

I prodded him for more information but he was quickly growing bored of the process. Kiara didn't raise her eyes from her iphone at any point in the process. She was furiously typing the entire time.

'Okay Darrell, do you want me to explain your interview options to you?' I asked, knowing full well that he knew his options as well as I did. He slouched further down the chair, with one hand down his pants. I really never understood why the majority of my youth male clients had a need to touch themselves at all times.

'Miss you know what I'm goin' to do innit-'no comment' all the way.' He knew that, that would have been my advice to him anyway. The only real evidence that the police had against him was that he was black and found in the vicinity of the robbery. The description given by the victim was so vague that there was no way it would support a charge. If Darrell refused to tell them anything, my guess was that no further action would be taken and he would walk out of the station sometime later this morning.

'Right Darrell, I just need you to sign some forms for me,' I said sliding the forms towards him which entitled him to free and independent legal advice. My representation today wouldn't cost him anything but the Legal Services Commission would pay our firm under the Legal Aid Scheme. He signed the forms with a scrawl. I knew that Darrell couldn't write properly, but all that was needed on these forms was some mark of a signature.

'Okay ready to go then?' I said looking from Darrell to Kiara.

She looked like she had been dosing and shook herself awake, blinking to get me into focus. 'Lets just get on with it,' she grunted, no doubt more annoyed at missing out on her beauty sleep than at her brother for being in police custody. Her role as an appropriate adult was to ensure that Darrell understood everything that was discussed at the interview. I couldn't imagine Kiara intervening if Darrell was having difficulty understanding something. My guess was she didn't even understand some of what was said at the interviews. Which was ironic considering that I knew that she had been arrested, interviewed and charged numerous times.

After a wait, the officers returned and the tapes were turned on. The preliminaries of name, address and the caution were dealt with and Darrell batted back 'no comment' replies to all of the officers questions. He was adept at not allowing the officers to trick him into answering their questions, despite their best efforts.

As the tapes were switched off, I knew with certainty that he would be out of here in a couple of hours. From his smirk, he knew the same and to confirm this he gave me a cocky little wink. Even though I knew that he was capable of being extremely violent I only ever saw the slightly cheeky side of him. As I left the custody suite I checked the time. I should get home by 6.45 No time for a snooze, I thought with disappointment. I drove home to Clapham on autopilot, already exhausted and the entire day stretched out before me.

CHAPTER TWO

As I pushed my way through the front door I almost barrelled into Laura who seemed in as much of a hurry to get out the door as I was to get in.

'Morning,' my voice chirped, sounding far more awake than I felt. Laura groaned. 'I fudging hate my life,' she muttered, tucking her blond hair behind her ears. Fudging was Laura's attempt to reduce her cursing. I had to hand it to her for remembering, when she was clearly half asleep and also having one of those mornings.

'I'm so fudging late. I'm supposed to be on a conference call in half an hour and I haven't properly prepped my notes. Oh is that coffee?' she said eyeing up my travel mug. Before I could stop her she had grabbed it and slugged as though her life depended on it. She grimaced as, the completely chilled coffee entered her mouth.

'Ugh why didn't you say it was cold? Anyway I'm late. Gotta run. Are you still up for gatecrashing our drinks later?' she yelled as she speed walked down the drive. I didn't bother replying as she was already out of earshot. Laura worked in Mergers and Acquisitions for a big firm in the city. Although we both worked in law, at times it felt like we existed in completely different worlds. She got into law because that was what her family did. I got into law because it seemed like a sound option. I wanted to earn good money and the careers adviser had said that because I was good at English it was an obvious choice. It really was a pity I hadn't stopped to think about this advice somewhere along the line. Anywhere from applying to universities to looking for a training contract would have been good. Instead now I was stuck on the lawtrain with no idea how to get off.

I checked the clock in the kitchen which told me it was 7.00am. It would be completely pointless crawling back into bed for a measly 15 minutes. The files for my court cases that day were staring at me from the coffee table in the sitting room. I decided to have a shower and prep them as I was having breakfast.

As I rifled through my wardrobe looking for an unwrinkled shirt, I phoned Battersea Police Station to check up on Darrell and to find out the result of his interview. I felt considerably refreshed after my shower and almost didn't feel as though I had only had two and a half hours sleep. As I was put on hold, I held up a shirt wondering if it was presentable. I really had to get stricter about ironing clothes I thought to myself. I gave it a good shake. I don't know why I always presumed that this got rid of the wrinkles. It didn't.

The Detention Officer came back on the line and informed me that Darrell had been released and no further action had been taken in his case. I allowed myself a little smile. One of these days they would be able to pin something big on Andrew but until that time he was back on the streets.

Back in the sitting room, I switched on the news as I was having my porridge and read my files for court that day. My ears perked up as I heard a reporter talking about more financial cuts to the legal aid system. 'What do they want us to do?' I muttered to myself, 'work for free?'

I was well aware that the money had to be squeezed from somewhere but it felt like soon I'd be financially better off if I worked in the supermarket around the corner. The talk on the news reminded me of an article I had read in the Law Gazette. The Government were looking at trying to develop a judicial system where the courts would be open 7 days a week. As far as I was aware none of my colleagues objected to this. However what was happening at the moment was that they were suggesting a pilot scheme in Manchester where they expected the solicitors to work for free on Saturdays and Sundays.

At the moment, firms were refusing to ask their employees to work for free on Saturdays and Sundays which was good news as far as I was concerned but it certainly didn't bode well for the future.

In the bathroom, I pulled my long hair into a ponytail and got to work on my makeup. Thank god for Touche Eclat! The circles under my eyes seemed a little less like craters after it was applied.

Grabbing my files, I stuffed them into my wheelie bag and as I headed out into the dark morning, I looked wistfully at my car. How nice it would be to hop in and drive to court in a civilised manner. However it was the crammed and steamy northern line for me. I used to enjoy the luxury of driving to court in the mornings but unfortunately due to more financial cuts by the Legal Services Commission, unless I could justify why I had to drive to court it was public transport for me. As much as I racked my brain I couldn't think of a valid reason why I would need to drive to Wimbledon Magistrates Court from Clapham.

At the tube station, I grabbed a copy of the Metro, swiped my oyster card and prepared for the crush.

CHAPTER THREE

'So do you work on Laura's team?' the drunk and slightly sweaty man slurred into my ear. This had also been his opening line to me when I had gate crashed one of Laura's work-dos about three months ago. His name was Henry and according to Laura the only reason he still worked there was because he was the star of the firm's rugby team.

His 6 foot 4 frame was now shifting unsteadily beside me but this didn't deter him from grabbing another drink from the passing waiter's tray. I looked down at my almost empty glass. 'Oh sorry, did you want one?' he questioned making a half hearted attempt to go after the waiter. 'Got to make full use of the free bar!' he guffawed. I shook my head but Henry seemed to have lost interest in my drink situation by this time and was back to wondering about my role within the firm. 'So what team are you on then?' he persisted. On paper Henry was a catch. Tall, blonde, a double barrelled name and very good looking. He ruined all this however once he began talking.

I caught Laura's eye. She was standing across the room stifling a yawn. It looked like her week of surviving on three or four hours sleep a night was catching up on her. Apparently they were almost at completion stage of a big deal and according to Laura her workload should lessen after this for a while, but in my experience these were famous last words. Laura winked at me, which I knew meant that she would be over to rescue me as soon as she could. But for the moment I was on my own. I returned my attention to Henry who was looking at me expectantly.

'I don't work with this firm. I'm a criminal defence lawyer.' I could see him almost physically recoil. 'Oh,' he said, seemingly stuck for words. 'Well then...' I could see his eyes travelling around the room looking for someone more interesting to talk to.

Like most law students I had been seduced by how a lawyer's life was portrayed in TV shows. While growing up I had been glued to LA law, Boston Legal and other glamorous programmes which seemed to suggest that a career as a lawyer promised glamorous Armani suits, offices decorated by an interior designer and above all a large pay packet.

As a student I discovered that criminal defence was the only area of law that interested me. I found all other areas dull and tedious. I also had the idealistic notion that If I chose this career path I would spend my days working for the down trodden and giving a voice to those who society had forgotten about. Unfortunately no-one had told me that with all the financial cuts being made I wouldn't earn enough to buy those Armani suits I had fallen in love with on TV. I usually kept the fact that some of my suits came from charity shops to myself. Although I suppose I could call them vintage to make them seem more palatable!

I, along with so many of my colleagues now regretted getting into criminal defence. I knew from listening to the talk around various advocates' rooms in London that many regretted not selling their souls to the city. However from living with Laura, I knew that far away hills were green. Despite my sometimes gruelling hours, the work was definitely not boring and I knew I did help people although probably not as much as I had expected when I had been studying.

On hearing about my career choice, Henry had rapidly lost interest in me and had wandered off in the direction of the bar. I stared miserably into my almost empty glass. 'Hey!' Laura greeted me. 'Why do you look so glum? Was Henry nasty to you?'

'No, I said. 'He just confirmed that even lawyers don't like criminal defence lawyers!' I tried to be light hearted about it but really what was getting me down was that his reaction was exactly how I felt at times. 'Don't let Henry get you down. Cheer up, it's Friday and you aren't on-call this weekend so you officially don't have to work for two whole days,' Laura said, ever the optimist. 'Thanks Laura,' I said, gratefully accepting the gin and tonic that she handed me. I squeezed the lemon into the liquid and stirred it with the straw.

'I think I'm probably going to leave in a bit to get the last tube home. Do you want to come then too?' she questioned. This was music to my ears. People were beginning to drift off by this time anyway and my lack of sleep last night was catching up on me.

'I'm ready to go now if you are?' I asked hopefully.

'Kate, my bed is calling to me. Let's go.'

As we went to locate our coats I felt my phone buzz in my bag. I pulled it out and saw that it was a text from Basil, my boss. My heart sank when I saw his name. I had a feeling that his text would have the potential to ruin my free weekend. Reluctantly I read through it. He wanted to know if I could cover a court hearing at City of Westminster Magistrates Court in the morning.

Apparently, a client of ours had been charged with Theft and Going Equipped for Theft and had been remanded at West End Central Police station until tomorrow morning when he would be brought to court. I thought about his question for a moment. Making a quick decision I text Basil back to say that I wouldn't be able to cover it as I already had plans. He didn't need to know that those plans involved catching up on some much needed sleep. I knew that if I attended Westminster in the morning there would be a good chance that I could be there for hours before the prosecution papers for my client would be available for me. The fixed fee I would receive for the attendance seemed almost unimportant when I could potentially be at court for almost all of Saturday.

The day fixed fees were introduced was a sad one for us lawyers. Older lawyers loved to regale us 'youngsters' about the 'good 'ol days' when a lot of money could be made in this profession. Sadly for me they were long gone. I knew that he would ask a 'baby barrister' to cover it. These were newly qualified barristers and always hungry for the experience.

As we were almost at the door, I spied Henry making his way towards us and I hurried Laura out into the crisp November air. I didn't see the point in missing the last tube home because we had been making inane conversation with him.

'Brrr,' Laura shivered. I knew that had Laura been on her own she probably would have hailed a cab to take her from the bar back to Clapham. Unfortunately, my salary didn't stretch beyond public transport, so both of us scurried towards the tube station. I really needed to find my gloves! I stuck my hands in the pocket of my coat as we walked quickly along, both of us lost in our own thoughts. I was grateful that Laura hadn't hinted at the possibility of us hailing a cab. There was a week to go until payday and as usual at this time of the month I was counting every penny. The free open bar at Laura's work party had been a major selling point for me. Even the finger food had seemed more appealing than usual. Cripes, anyone listening to my thoughts would think I was a broke student and not a working lawyer.

'Did you have fun?' Laura asked as we hopped onto the tube. 'Sorry I kind of abandoned you but I was a bit hypnotised by 'hot guys' eyes.

'Hot guy', was actually called Matt and he seemed

to have that effect on most girls. Consequentially he had probably slept with most of the attractive females in Laura's office. For some reason however Laura seemed to think that she would be different. I suspected that all the other girls had thought the same.

'I know you think I'm silly for lusting after him but really it's just a bit of fun. It's the first time since Dave broke up with me that I've been able to even *think* about another guy,' she proclaimed. Her blue eyes looked in danger of welling up. Dave had been her first and only long-term boyfriend. They had met in college and had been together for about seven years. Everyone had expected them to get engaged but instead they ended up breaking up. Poor Laura had cried herself to sleep for weeks and she had had real difficulty accepting Dave's explanation that he had simply fallen out of love with her. I supposed that I should be more encouraging of her moving on. Even if it was with the office Lothario.

'Hey,' I said as we headed to the tube station exit. 'I think it's fabulous that you are moving on. I honestly do. You deserve some fun.' This was definitely the truth. In fact I think I deserved some fun too I thought self indulgently. Of late both of our lives seemed to involve working far too much and not sleeping enough.

'Fudge it,' Laura exclaimed, breaking through my thoughts, as we reached our front door. I had to hand it to her. She really was making headway with trying not to curse.

'I've left my keys on my desk at work. Do you have yours?' she asked anxiously. I rummaged in my bag, produced a key and as usual struggled with the door lock before throwing myself at it, to push it open. 'Stupid door,' I muttered, as I fell into the hallway.

'Jesus it's freezing in here, we really have to sort out the timer on the heating,' I said not for the first time this winter. We both knew that unless we actually drove to our landlord's house, smuggled him into my car and back to our house that it would remain unfixed. Actually even if we did succeed in getting him here it was highly likely that he wouldn't be able to do anything about it. Although he called himself a handyman, really the only thing Bob seemed handy for was accepting our rent direct debits every month.

'I'm exhausted,' Laura said sleepily, as she dragged herself upstairs. I'll see you in the morning.'

'Night night, I said as my phone buzzed. It was another text from Basil. It read-

'Any chance you could change your plans tomorrow? I'm finding it difficult to find cover for court?'

Anger rose up inside me. Change my plans! How dare he, I thought indignantly. Why couldn't he get off his fat arse and cover it himself I wondered. I checked the time. It was now 1am. If I was to attend court this morning I would have to be up at 7.30am. I had been so looking forward to a sleep in. I knew I could refuse to attend but really I could do with the money. I'm sure I'd appreciate it when it hit my bank account next month. Sometimes I just had to force myself to do the out of hours work as very often this was what got me through to the next payday. I decided to swallow my indignation.

I groaned in defeat and text Basil back.

Ok. I can attend. Can you please forward on clients details to me. Thanks.

As I brushed my teeth I looked at myself in the mirror. I swear I was aging faster than I should be. In five years time I'd probably look 40 instead of 34 I thought sadly. I must start doing the euro millions I thought to myself as I curled up in bed. I fell asleep listing the things I would do if I won it. The first thing on my list was to quit my job and tell Basil exactly what I thought of him.

CHAPTER FOUR

The following morning I walked past Starbucks on my way to court. The door swung open as someone exited and the familiar aroma of coffee filled my nostrils. I was painfully aware of the tiny balance left in my bank account and of the number of days left until I got paid. I stood procrastinating for a couple of moments before pushing the door open. I needed some enjoyment in my day I reasoned with myself.

As I stood in line contemplating whether to get a Tall or Grande sized coffee my heart almost skipped a beat. As corny as that phrase is it most definitely applied to how I felt, when I saw Alex smile at the barista who was fluttering her heavily made up lashes at him. He moved towards the pick-up area and as he turned around, I knew that he had spotted me.

I could feel my cheeks warm. I gave him what I hoped was a smile but I had a feeling that it looked more like a smirk. Why was I always so awkward around men that I found attractive, I sighed inwardly. I really was a lost cause. I had only had one, as my Mum described him 'proper boyfriend' in all my 29 years. His name was Paul and he had moved to live in Australia, leaving me behind and distraught. Apparently he needed to find himself in the big bad world. Alone. That had been when I was 25 and I suppose you could say I was having a bit of a dry spell on the manfront, since then. Although after 4 years I suppose it was more of a desert than a dry spell.

Alex was a barrister at Fernhouse chambers and did a lot of work for our firm. I was also insanely attracted to him. I was five foot 10, which sometimes meant I ended up literally looking down on guys. However, his 6 foot 4 frame always felt masculine beside me. He had dark, curlyish hair, a broad build and looked fabulous in a suit.

'Would you like that for here or to go?' the barista asked, jerking me back to reality. Funnily she didn't seem as friendly with me as she had done with Alex. 'Em to go,' I stuttered.

'Kate, long time no-see,' Alex exclaimed strolling towards me, holding a Venti sized cup in his hand. Be cool, be cool, I urged myself mentally. How by the age of 29 had I not developed the ability to speak to men I fancied in a normal manner? Maybe I had some permanent, psychological scars from Paul. Maybe I needed to see a psychologist. Kate get a grip, I scolded myself.

'Alex, great to see you,' I smiled. Excellent I congratulated myself. 'Are you in court this morning?' I asked. Stupid question, I chided myself. Of course he was going to court. I took in his suit and briefcase.

'Yes, I've got an over-nighter. Charged with GBH. You?'

'Theft and Going Equipped for Theft. A Romanian male.'

God he was cute. He held the door open and we walked out into the crisp air. I racked my brain for something to say that would make me sound incredibly funny and desirable. Beating me to it he asked if I had seen the new legal aid cuts proposed in the recent paper published by the Ministry of Justice. Not the scintillating conversation I had been hoping for but at least we were talking.

'We'll be bloody working for free soon,' he exclaimed in his public school tones before taking a sip of his coffee.

'I know,' I said miserably, thinking of all the years I had studied to become a lawyer, always envisioning that at the end I would be financially secure. This couldn't be further from the reality of my situation. By the time my college loans and rent were paid every month I was left with just enough money for food and the odd indulgence.

'Sorry-I didn't mean to depress you,' he said, as he noticed me lost in my own thoughts. 'So,' he said no doubt in an attempt to lighten the mood 'will you be coming to our chambers Christmas party?' he smiled, before taking a long drink of his coffee. I tried to decipher this question. Did he really care whether I attended the party or was he just speaking so as we wouldn't be walking in silence. I knew that *of course* I would be attending their party. I even knew what I would be wearing. It had been Laura's suggestion actually. I had been lamenting about the fact that I couldn't afford to buy a new dress for the round of parties in December and Laura had offered that I could wear the dress she had worn to her office party last Christmas. However Alex didn't need to know that I was this enthusiastic about the event.

'Em, yes I'm going,' I said nonchalantly. He didn't have a chance to reply as we had reached the court lobby and I handed my bag to the security guard so he could pass it through the scanner. He gestured at my coffee cup. Sighing, I pulled the top off and showed him that it was indeed coffee and not some chemical concoction designed to blow up the building.

We both walked towards the board, which would tell us which courtroom our cases would be heard in. I scanned through the list of over-nighters, so called as they had spent the night in Police custody at the station. My client would be appearing in courtroom 4 and Alex's case would be dealt with in courtroom 5.

'I'll see you later Kate. I'm crossing my fingers and hoping to get out of here as soon as possible so as I can enjoy some of my weekend,' Alex said as he headed up the stairs. 'Good luck,' he added as he disappeared up to the next level.

I would need luck. My case was listed in front of District Judge Farmer who was notoriously tough. Oh well I thought to myself, I had better get on with it. I headed towards the stairs. The only plus side of Saturday court sittings was the relative calm at court. It was only custody cases that were listed so the halls were generally very quiet.

CHAPTER FIVE

I walked into courtroom four and went to speak to the prosecutor, who was standing hunched over the bench, sorting through her files for this morning. I wanted to obtain the papers for my client, Mr. Albu's case. Unfortunately we would need a Romanian interpreter and the list-caller had informed me that one had not turned up yet. It was the responsibility of the police to book an interpreter but at the moment due to pay cuts, many interpreters were striking and refusing to attend court.

The prosecutor turned to face me and as I approached her, her hollow eyes told me that she needed sleep. Her lips were set in a straight line and I figured she wanted to be here about as much as I did.

'Morning,' I said cheerily. My encounter with Alex had brightened my mood. 'I'm looking for the papers for Mr. Albu,' I said as I directed a megawatt smile in her direction. I crossed my fingers willing them to be on the bench in front of her. Wordlessly, she turned and after searching and rummaging through all her files, she produced what I needed. I sighed with relief. Thankfully the papers had arrived at court on time.

Unfortunately this was not the norm. I took the papers from the prosecutor and headed towards the Advocates room to read them. Juggling my coffee cup, bag and the file, I entered the access code on the keypad beside the door. As I walked in, I nodded politely to two gentlemen who were seated at the large round table chatting and drinking coffee. I settled down to read the papers, while also doing a bit of eavesdropping on their conversation. They seemed to be talking about some rugby star who was dating someone from the girlband FAB. I had to hide a grin.

Listening to their conversation they could have been any two teenage girls having a gossip! From what I could gather the girl had posed for some lads mag recently and the boyfriend wasn't too happy about it and had dumped her. As they continued to talk I realised that the dumpee hadn't taken it all very well and that she had scratched his Audi car yesterday afternoon causing somewhere in the region of £1200 of damage. It turned out that the older of the two men had represented her at Charing Cross police station yesterday, where she had been interviewed for criminal damage. I wondered what she looked like after spending some time in a police cell.

I had previously represented a soapstar who had spent a night in custody after a very drunken incident in Soho where she had attacked a bouncer with a bottle after he had refused her entry into a club. After the don't you know who I am card? had failed she had decided in her drunken state that the only option available to her was to bottle him. When I met her the next morning at the Police station she was in a right state. Her blonde hair was matted to her head and I could clearly see where her extensions had been put in. Her eyes were blood shot and her skimpy dress from the night before revealed orange patchy fake tan. It was definitely a different image to the one she portrayed to the media. After seeing her like that I reckoned that anyone could look pretty decent if they had a stylist, make-up artist and hairdresser at their disposal.

I really was such a day dreamer. I pulled out the papers for today's client and scanned through them. The modus operandi in today's case seemed almost identical to all the other thefts I had dealt with in previous weeks where the perpetrator had been Romanian. Very recently large numbers were coming to London, on long bus journeys. Some were coming with the hope of a better life for themselves. However others were coming in as part of a gang. They were either living homeless or in houses where it wasn't unusual to find up to four sharing a small cramped room. They lined their bags with tin-foil, in order to avoid the security detectors, and headed off into London's shops and tubes to steal as much as they could. Very often they would then wire the proceeds of their 'work' back to their family in Romania.

When they were caught, they invariably required interpreters and once charged were kept in custody for court the following morning. The police generally had substantial grounds to believe that if given police bail to surrender to the courts at a later date, they would abscond.

Mr. Albu had gone with his foil-lined bag into a John Lewis store and was seen on CCTV and by store security guards, to be acting in a suspicious manner before putting four jumpers into the bag he was carrying. He was stopped as he was leaving the store and searched. Police were called and he was arrested. It was a textbook theft case. I guessed that he didn't know that the CCTV in England was very efficient. Also the fact that he was Romanian, made him a prime target for the beady eyes of store detectives.

At the station he had been represented by Nick, one of my colleagues from the office and had been assisted by a Romanian interpreter. He had admitted to the Theft and Going Equipped for the Theft with the tin-foil lined bag in interview so I anticipated a guilty plea at today's hearing. Unfortunately I couldn't do anything without the interpreter. I stood deciding to go to the cells anyway to see whether he had any English at all.

As I was buzzed through to the custody suite, I could hear high pitched screaming coming from one of the cells. Very often there was someone who screamed and shouted for the entire time they were in custody. Even if this was for a full day. Some had reasons such as they needed their drug fix, others had mental health problems but others just did it to annoy the detention officers.

I signed in, trying to block out the high pitched wailing noise. I asked to speak with Mr. Albu. The detention officers gestured at me to take a consultation room. I chose one without a glass screen between us. Unless the detention officers specifically felt that a client was dangerous I preferred to have my consultations in a normal room. As I walked towards interview room six I breathed in the stale air. I sat waiting for him.

When he entered I could get a strong unwashed smell from him and as he got closer I could see the dirt under his finger nails. His face and hands had a weathered look. He wore a black jumper and dirty jeans which did little to hide his thin frame.

I told him my name and asked him his. He stared at me blankly. 'English?' I enquired. 'Romanian,' he said, rolling the 'R'.

'We wait for interpreter,' I said slowly, having no idea whether he understood me or not.

'Yes. Yes, interpreter,' he said shaking his head enthusiastically. Obviously he had understood my pidgin English. I gestured with my hands that I was going to go and find one and he continued nodding eagerly. I left the cells, told the detention officers that I was finished and went to check on whether our interpreter had arrived at court yet.

As I was climbing the stairs, it crossed my mind that in recent months, this had become the extent of my exercise regime. I had been so into working out and now unfortunately it seemed that all I did was work.

The list caller for my court was sitting in an almost empty courtroom, doodling on a piece of paper. She looked up as I approached. 'Miss, yours is the last case left to be called on.' I checked my watch. It was almost lunchtime. No doubt DJ Farmer wanted to be elsewhere for his Saturday afternoon rather than sitting on the bench in court. 'Regrettably, there's not a lot I can do I'm afraid. We really can't proceed without the interpreter. I was just down in the cells with him and he says he needs one. Why don't you call his case on and I can explain this to the Judge?' I suggested.

I went to sit at the defence advocates position, shuffling my papers and rising to bow at the Judge when he eventually entered. He looked very pissed off, I observed. Everyone looked towards Mr. Albu who had been brought up from his cell by two detention officers. His handcuffs were removed and he stood behind the glass screen. He looked confused.

'Miss Hunter,' the judge said addressing me. I stood, 'Yes, Sir?'

'I understand that your client requires a Romanian interpreter, which we are sadly lacking at court today. Is that correct?'

'Yes sir.' I went on to explain that I had met with him in the cells and that a consultation had been impossible due to the fact that my knowledge of the Romanian language was nonexistent.

'Well then, Miss Hunter, I don't see any alternative but to keep him in custody until Monday morning when he will hopefully have the services of an interpreter.'

'But Sir,' I interrupted.

'Miss Hunter, I have remanded him in custody until Monday. My decision has been made. We cannot make any progress today.'

'Sir, may I address you on the issue of bail?' I questioned, knowing full well that the Judge would not entertain such an application and in any event it would be impossible to make a bail application as I had not been able to take instructions from Mr. Albu. Out of the corner of my eye, I had seen my client perk up slightly at the mention of the word bail so I suspected that he knew more English than he was letting on. He appeared to be nodding. My main reason for asking for bail was to keep the client happy. Well as happy as he could be, being detained in prison for the weekend. Very often we ended up making applications which we knew had little or no hope of succeeding simply because it was what our client instructed us to do or it was what would make them happy. Despite advising clients against making such applications they often ignored us and we had to make a wholehearted attempted at a futile application. Sometimes I became so convinced by my own argument half way through that I was almost shocked when the Judge or Magistrate refused it.

'I trust you will make an effort to explain this to your client Miss Hunter,' the judge stated before rising and making a hasty exit. I picked up my papers and walked dejectedly towards the cells preparing to speak pidgin English once more. Unfortunately as I hadn't been able to speak with my client and obtain his instructions, getting his signature on the forms required for Legal Aid had not been possible. As defence lawyers, we hated those forms. All too often we attended court, like I had today and because for one reason or another we had been unable to get one of the many lengthy legal aid forms signed we were not paid for our attendance. I guessed that very few professions would work for free or in the vain hope that they would get paid. They didn't tell us about this in college I thought wryly.

I searched through my folders trying to find a legal aid form which I thought I might be able to submit to entitle our firm to payment for today. Unfortunately I only seemed to have CDS 14 and CDS 15s with me. These were the most frequently used forms and in excess of 10 pages each. Filling them out for every client quickly grew tiresome. 'Damn,' I muttered to myself. Basil would not be happy with me.

Once again in the cells, I was faced with Mr. Albu.

'No Interpreter today,' I began slowly.

'No interpreter?' he said, looking panicked. His eyes were wide and his mouth open.

'Monday,' I said hurriedly, trying to prevent an emotional outburst from him. 'Interpreter on Monday,' I repeated slowly, enunciating the words clearly.

'Me, what happen me?' he questioned. His eyes were wide. This was going brilliantly I thought wryly to myself. I was discovering though that his command of the English language seemed a lot better than he had previously let on.

'You, prison, until Monday,' I said slowly, pointing my hands at him and then towards the detention officer. Miraculously he seemed to grasp what I was saying.

'Ahh okay, what happen Monday?' he stuttered in heavily accented English.

'Monday, back here with interpreter,' I said drawing out the words.

'Okay. Okay, he said nodding his head in understanding. His acceptance of his situation didn't surprise me. Very often I met with clients who were perfectly happy to spend some time in prison as they really didn't have anywhere else to go. It was their reasoning that at least they were being fed and kept warm in prison. Many considered it safer than the streets.

As I left the building I breathed in the chilled air. I felt relieved to be leaving at lunchtime. Suddenly the world

31

seemed at rights again. A full day and a half of no work stretched hopefully ahead of me. I felt content.

Before I let myself get into the weekend mode too much I sent Basil a quick text.

Client charged with Theft-Romanian-no interpreter-remanded until Monday-do you want me to attend?

I pressed send and knew that at some point today I would receive a text about the legal aid situation. I sighed. Well there was nothing I could do about it now.

As I walked towards the tube my phone rang. I expected the call to be from Basil but I smiled when I saw the name ' Lil Sis' flash up.

'Sis, how's it going?' I answered.

'Siswa!' she said in reply. That was our affectionate name for each other. Even our older brother James, sometimes called us Siswa. I pulled my wheelie bag to the side of the pavement so as I wouldn't have to walk and talk.

'I'm just at the airport,' she continued, without pausing for breath. That's right. She was heading to New York for a 4 day break with her boyfriend. She had been planning on doing a little sightseeing and a lot of shopping. Sis loved shopping as much as I did but luckily for her, her job in banking allowed her to indulge her addiction. It was slightly depressing when my younger sister had more money than I did.

'Anyway,' she said, 'It's Dad's 60th in January and I was wondering if you had any ideas of what we could get him?' We always chipped together to get our parents presents, but this year it would have to be something special, being his 60th.

'Em...how about a big box of love!' I said not entirely joking. I had serious cashflow problems at the moment and I would have to do more out of hours work in order to get the money to buy his present. Even thinking like this however made me feel like a selfish daughter. What was a few extra hours work, considering everything he had done for me during my life?

'I really don't know Sis,' I said hastily, before she could call me out for being a mean spirited and ungrateful daughter. 'You are generally really good with ideas so how about you buy whatever you think he'd like and I'll give you the money when you're back?'

'That's perfect Siswa. Oh they're calling our flight. I gotta dash. Chat soon,' she sing songed. I didn't have a chance to wish her a good trip before she rang off.

CHAPTER SIX

Monday morning came around all too quickly and once again I was at the mercy of the alarm clock. As I rolled out of bed my mind began thinking about my day ahead. I was at City of Westminster Magistrates Court again this morning to deal with Mr. Albu and I also had two other clients. As I was putting my make-up on, I thought of Alex and hoped that he would be at court as well today. With that in mind I put on a little extra mascara. Having a lust interest definitely made going to work more manageable!

As I got ready to leave the house, I tucked my high-heels into my big black wheelie bag. I hated having to wheel this around London, up and down tube steps and generally putting my back out. There really was no other way of getting all my files around though. Most days I looked like I was going on holidays as I left the house. I always envied the girls who skipped around with only a handbag swinging from their arm. As I pulled the wheelie bag over the bumpy ground I looked longingly in at the numerous coffee shops I passed. I would have loved a coffee but I was trying to reduce the amount I was drinking. At the moment I felt jittery if I didn't have it and jittery if I drank too much of it which I figured couldn't be good for me.

On the tube, for some miraculous reason, I got a seat. As I sat there I began to think of my Dad and his birthday. It had upset me more than I had let on to Sis that I would really struggle to donate to his present. I knew feeling sorry for myself wasn't going to get me anywhere, but I sometimes felt so helpless. I knew I needed to change my job, if I wanted to have slightly more money. That was precisely the problem though. I didn't know what else I could do and it made me feel incredibly trapped. I could see thirty more years of this life looming ahead and it scared the hell out of me.

As I left the tube, I made an effort to leave my misery behind me in the carriage. There was no point in starting the week in a state of despair.

'Well Miss Hunter,' I heard a voice behind me say. My heart leapt as I recognised the posh tones. ' You *are* a striking figure in that blue coat.'

I didn't want to let him know how pleased I was that he had said this. I had agonised for days about whether or not to buy this coat. It was my favourite midnight blue colour, came to my knee and fitted snugly. It had meant that in October, I had pretty much been eating the proverbial beans on toast for the last week of the month. There really isn't a lot that can be done to make beans on toast exciting and believe me I'd tried. I had trawled through the internet for recipes on how to jazz them up. I'd discovered that there really is a gap in the market there!

'Why, thank you Mr. Grant,' I said with a smile. 'Anything interesting today?' I asked as we passed through security.

'A burglary trial with four co-defendants. We have a five day listing so I'll be here all week.'

I absorbed this nugget of information about his whereabouts for the rest of the week. I wonder could I engineer some more hearings at this court I mused. Although I was considering myself lucky to be here today. Westminster Magistrates court was a newly opened building and had glossy, new fixtures and fittings. Some of the other courts around London were grotty, cold, run-down and really rather depressing buildings to be spending a lot of time in. It often amused me now, when I watched law programmes on TV at how different the courtrooms in those series appeared. I suppose TV ratings may not be as high if they showed the reality of the situation.

My phone ringing bought me back to the present. Alex did some strange sign with his hand that I took to mean that he would talk to me later. The screen told me it was a blocked number. I hated answering blocked numbers as it was invariably a police station calling. I pressed the answer button. 'Hello, Miss Hunter speaking.' After a moment I repeated myself as no-one had answered me back. There was silence on the other end. I hung up the phone. Whoever it was could phone back if it was important I decided.

I turned my attention to Alex who had busied himself on the other side of the advocate's room and was looking through his notes for today's trial. I took off my ballet flats and wiggled my feet into my heels. For some reason I felt far more professional and authoritative when wearing them. It was as if they transferred me into work mode. Obviously they made my legs look longer as well, which was always a bonus, particularly when Alex was in such close proximity.

My phone rang again with the words 'blocked' written on the screen. This time I ignored it. Whoever it was would have to leave a message. I sorted through my files in my wheelie bag and grabbed the three that were listed for this morning. Out of the corner of my eye I could see Alex chatting with some other blonde advocate. They were pouring over case files, their heads bent close together. I presumed that she was one of his co-defending lawyers. I felt a pang of envy. I would love to be working with Alex for the week. We could go for lunch together and maybe even have a coffee after court. My mind drifted to the conversations we would have. Before I could get too caught up in fantasy, I dragged myself back to earth. I would be spending my morning with an alcoholic, a Romanian and someone who went by the name of Mr. Jacobs. I left the advocates room, forcing myself not to look towards the back of the room as I exited. I really think I had a bad case of Alexitis.

I headed towards the courtrooms and checked myself in with the listcaller. I then went in search of Mr. Vincente. He was a regular client of ours. He had a terrible drinking problem and most of his convictions were as a result of his inability to know when to stop. I walked towards him knowing instinctively he had been drinking already this morning.

'Good morning Mr. Vincente,' I said cheerily. 'You're looking well,' I added, sitting down beside him. I regretted this immediately as the smell of body odour and alcohol hit my nostrils.

'You're too kind dear,' he slurred. If the smell of beer from his breath didn't give away that he had been drinking his slurred speech certainly did. He lived on the streets when things soured with his wife and then would move back in when she forgave him. From the layer of dirt covering his skin, his bloodshot eyes and hunched shoulders I guessed that he was living on the streets at the moment. It was terribly sad but there were hundreds more like him who lived in volatile domestic situations who spent their time either at home, on the streets or in prison.

However I had to remind myself that the reason that he was living on the streets was that he had a tendency to drink to excess and take any anger he was feeling out on his wife. I had previously been involved in a case where he had punched her twice to the face and then begun to throw household items such as glasses, vases and cutlery at her. She had spent two weeks in hospital after that assault. Despite this she kept taking him back.

This time he was appearing in court for something less serious. He had been drinking and then wandered around Marble Arch screaming at people and now he faced a charge under the Public Order Act. I read through his interview summary with him, where he had chosen to be unrepresented by a solicitor. When interviewed, he had said that he was having a conversation with the pigeons and that he hadn't been speaking to the people at all and therefore he wasn't guilty of the offence as clearly a pigeon couldn't provide a statement of complaint to the police. I had to hide a smile. He did have a point.

'So Mr. Vincente, what are you saying about this matter today?' I questioned. Mr. Vincente always knew what he wanted to do. He had been in and out of courts for most of his life and knew how to play the system without needing legal advice. I suspected that he was lonely and sometimes he just wanted a lawyer so as he could talk to someone.

'Well Miss,' he began. It was hard to believe that the man sitting in front of me, who appeared gentle and almost gracious could be capable of violence which would put someone in hospital. He had caused so much injury to his brother once, that he had lost an eye. For that offence he had obtained a two year custodial sentence but, as under the English legal system only half of that had to be served he was out after a year.

'I suppose really the pigeon story wouldn't really hold up at trial if I went 'not guilty' today would it?'

I tried to keep a straight face and pretend that I was seriously considering his question. The fact that he had shouted 'You f**king black nigger, F*ck off home' would probably suggest that it was shouted at the black complainant who had provided a statement to the police and not at the pigeons.

'I'd probably be better off just getting it over and done with today eh? Get my credit for entering an early guilty plea eh?'

Mr. Vincente knew full well that if he pleaded guilty

at today's hearing he would get a third off his sentence.

'I think that's the correct thing to do Mr. Vincente. Now can you just sign these legal aid forms for me? Are you getting your benefits at the moment?'

'Yes Miss, JSA, picked it up yesterday in fact.'

I ticked the relevant box and we went on to fill out the rest of the form together.

'How long 'til we get on Miss?' he asked when we had finished filling out the lengthy form. If I had a pound for everytime I was asked this question, I thought to myself. Clients were always eager to get their cases called on as quickly as possible. Many failed to understand that even though they were told to be at court for 9.30am their case may not be called on for many hours after that. I hated when they took it out on me, as though it was my fault. Sometimes it was down to the fact that the case was listed in front of Magistrates instead of a District Judge. As they didn't have any formal legal training they relied heavily on advice from the legal advisor who sat in front of them. As a result they were usually very slow at making decisions with regards to sentence. Other times it could just be as simple as the court list being very long or that the Prosecution didn't have defence papers available at court so no progress could be made until these arrived. Really it could be one of many reasons why it was moving so slowly.

'You know my answer to that Mr. Vincente. Yes you have time to go outside for a cigarette but you can't go to the pub. Stay around this floor once you come back up and I'll try and get you on and out of here as soon as possible ok?'

'I knew you'd say that Miss,' he said with a gap-toothed smile. It really was a pity that he could never stick with his Alcohol Treatment Requirement programmes which had been handed down to him as sentences numerous times. As much as he wanted to get off drink he wanted to drink more. As a result he was constantly in and out of prison, which I suspected he didn't mind. I think he almost found the routine inside comforting.

As I walked away to check whether the Romanian interpreter had turned up for court I could see Mr. Vincente walking hastily towards the stairs to go for a cigarette. I glanced at my phone which showed that I had a message from Laura.

Fancy doing a take-away tonight? I need some girl time with chats. I could be out of here at 7.30 so home for 8.30ish?

It sounded great. I figured that there was only 5 more days until payday so I could spring to it.

Sounds fab. Count me in. Yum yum!

Did I ever think when I was studying that I would consider a takeaway a splurge when I was qualified and working?

I also had a voicemail from that blocked number but I'd listen to that later. As I scanned the list for the interpreters who had arrived at court, I saw that there were Polish, Spanish, Urdu and Mandarin interpreters in the building but sadly no Romanian interpreter yet. Mr. Albu would have to wait a little longer I supposed.

I checked with the list-caller whether my third client, Mr. Jacobs had turned up for court.

'No and I want to call the matter on next,' she replied.

I checked the time. It was 11.25am. I didn't have a contact number for him so had no way of finding out whether he had a reason for not attending court. He should have been at court about two hours ago so really there wasn't a lot I could say to convince the list-caller to hold on.

'I'm ready with Mr. Vincente,' I told her. 'Could

that be called on after Mr. Jacobs case?'

CHAPTER SEVEN

Later that day, as I was thinking that Mr. Albu would have served a full sentence by the time an interpreter showed up, I remembered the voicemail on my phone. As I pressed the listen button I waited to hear a police officer's voice. Instead I just heard silence. I took the phone from my ear to check that I had pressed the right button but the screen told me that it was playing as recorded. Weird, I thought. I hung up and checked the time on the phone. I decided to go and look again for this seemingly mythical interpreter. It was 3.30pm and one should really be arriving soon if we were to get the matter on today. Traditionally the courts finished at 4pm but more and more often I was finding myself still at court at 5pm and sometimes even later.

I walked towards the courtroom trying to locate the list caller. The courthouses were generally much quieter places in the afternoons as the throngs of people who attended either to answer their own bail or to accompany others had usually thinned. Today however there was obviously an overspill from the morning listing as there was still a bit of a buzz around and advocates were still walking around trying to find clients.

The list caller approached me as I neared the courtroom. 'Miss, I've just heard that there has been some sort of mix up with the interpreter's office and one won't be coming this afternoon.'

'This is ridiculous,' I muttered to myself. 'Someone cannot be held in custody for that length of time simply because our system is so inefficient that someone can't organize a phone call to book an interpreter.' Having delivered her message, the list-caller scurried away, obviously afraid that I was going to take my anger out on her.

I took a deep breath and decided to head towards the cells. Maybe Mr. Albu has learnt some English over the weekend in jail. I asked the jailers to bring him to me in a consultation room and I sat there wondering how I was going to communicate with him. When he walked in, he looked remarkably cleaner than on Saturday morning. In fact he looked a lot more cheerful. This probably had a lot to do with the fact that he had been fed three meals a day over the weekend. I suspected from his skinny frame that he often didn't have enough food to eat.

'Interpreter?' he questioned immediately, looking hopeful as he sat before me. He had obviously availed of the prisons full cleaning facilities as he didn't smell at all.

'No....interpreter....today...' I said in my drawn out Pidgin English.

His face dropped.

'I come for better life,' he said morosely, clasping his scrawny hands on the table.

Stunned by this relatively fluent outburst I kept quiet hoping that more would come.

'My wife and child stay in Romania.'

Now his eyes had taken on a pleading look and he was gesturing with his hands. I noticed that the grime had been washed from underneath his fingernails. I saw the look in his eyes that I saw in many who I met with in custody. They saw me as the hope which could make their predicament better. Unfortunately for Mr. Albu, given the strength of the evidence against him, I felt that a custodial sentence was almost inevitable. It was his first offence here in this country but unfortunately for him he was appearing in City of Westminster Magistrates Court. It was notorious for tough sentences, particularly for this type of offence. The courts were very obviously getting tired of Romanians appearing before them and were taking a hard line on sentencing.

However had he appeared before another London court he may have been lucky enough to get away with a fine. I had appeared in front of a bench of three Magistrates at Lavender Hill Magistrates Court near Clapham Junction last week. My client had only been in London for three months and already had three previous convictions for theft. He had received a fine for each of these offences. When he appeared before them last week for his fourth theft offence in three months, I was almost certain that he would get a custodial sentence. I warned him that this was a possibility but I had decided to invite the court to consider fining him.

I had almost laughed when I had said the words. However after spending some time deliberating the Magistrates decided to fine him for a fourth time. I couldn't believe it! He must be the luckiest Romanian to ever hit London. The ironic thing was that the Magistrates then became aware of the fact that he had not paid any of his fines for his previous offences. What made them think that he would now begin to pay off the fines was beyond me.

I didn't think that Mr. Albu would be so lucky.

I encouraged him to continue speaking by nodding my head up and down. I had found that this generally helped clients believe that I was on their side and they began to talk more freely.

'I come here to look for work. No work so I steal. I not bad man.'

I decided to try and throw in a question and went for the kernel of the matter.

'Did you steal the jumpers from John Lewis?' I asked slowly.

'Yes. Hungry. I need money.'

I decided against asking him whether he was part of a large gang who had proactively come to London for the purpose of stealing. It wouldn't do him any good if I was to tell the court this. Anyway the court would draw its own conclusions about why he had come here.

I went on to ask him questions about his personal situation so I could tell the court a little about him. I warned him that he would probably receive a custodial sentence but that as he was pleading guilty today he would get credit for this.

'How long prison?' he asked. Now that we had had a little chat he had visibly relaxed.

'Perhaps between 12-15 weeks initially, but you would possibly receive 8-10 weeks with credit for your early guilty plea. Then you would be released after serving half the sentence, so you could be out on licence in about 5 weeks.' I went on to explain what being on licence meant.

'When you are released early from prison in the UK you are put on licence. This means that if you commit another offence before the period of your sentence is up, your sentence will be activated and you will be recalled to prison.'

He almost looked happy.

'That ok. I nowhere to go. Food in prison.' I smiled sympathetically at him.

It was terrible that someone had such a poor personal situation that prison was a happy alternative. However, lately some of the media had been reporting that they were having difficulty accepting the fact that English taxpayers were spending a lot of money on keeping people like Mr. Albu in prison. They seemed to suggest that people should be sent back to whatever country they came from when they were convicted. Inevitably when they were then released from prison they disappeared into English cities. As they didn't have any money they usually resorted to petty crime in order to survive. It really appeared to be a vicious cycle.

I had been so idealistic when I was a student. I thought as lawyers we could make a difference and if I'm honest earn a lot of money doing it. However I usually felt like a hamster caught on a wheel. All I could do for Mr. Albu today was to try and get the best outcome for him. I had finally realised that there was little I could do to improve his life. My heart really went out to him and so many others like him. However I was powerless to make any real difference in his situation.

After asking Mr Albu if he was happy for his case to be called on without an interpreter I explained what would happen once he was bought up into court and the sentencing guidelines which the court would have to follow.

As I left court that day lugging my wheelie bag behind me, my mind wandered to the days happenings. Mr. Vincente had been given an appointment with the Probation services to see whether he was suitable for another Alcohol Treatment Programme. The Magistrates had said the famous words, we're giving you one last chance, Mr. Vincente. I had probably heard this twice before when representing him. He really was like a cat with nine lives. If I was to guess the result I would think that Mr. Vincente wasn't going to turn up for the appointment which would allow the probation services to access his suitability for the programme. If he turned up for his sentencing hearing at all he would probably get a short custodial sentence. As for my Mr. Albu, he had received a 12 week custodial sentence of which he would serve 6. He had seemed happy with this.

Cripes I was exhausted. Dealing with other people's problems all day was so tiring! Sometimes I felt like a social worker more than a lawyer. I checked the time on my phone. It was 5pm. The temptation to head straight home was huge but I had a feeling that Basil wouldn't appreciate it if I did. Even though it would probably be 5.30 by the time I got back to the office I really could do with catching up with some paper work. Well at least Monday was almost over and I had a night in with Laura to look forward to. Even though we lived together we actually didn't get to spend that much time hanging out due to our work hours.

Cheered by the thought of my nice night in, I headed towards Baker Street tube station so as I could head to my office near Chancery Lane. I pulled out my phone to send a text to Laura.

Leaving court now. Heading to the office for a bit but will leave at about 7-7.30ish so see you at home ☺

I pushed the send button before I headed into the station.

Sitting on the tube I closed my eyes while keeping one hand on the handle of my wheelie case. For some reason I was always paranoid that someone was going to run off with my files and that Basil would go mental. I could just imagine his fat face reddening as he pushed his glasses up on his nose. This was his default action when he was annoyed/furious/frustrated or really any emotion other than happy which he never seemed to be. I smiled to myself thinking how disappointed someone would be if they had gone to the trouble of stealing a bag, presuming it to be full of clothes or at the very least stuff that was in some way valuable. Then when they opened it all they would find was useless paper.

CHAPTER EIGHT

As I hauled my suitcase up the steps to our office building I almost collided with Nick who I shared an office with.

'Long time no see stranger!'

'I know. Have you missed me?' I grinned at him.

'My life just hasn't been the same,' he batted back.

'Where are you off to in such a hurry?' I questioned. He really was a good looking man. Tall, blond hair and a smile that got him out of many a sticky situation.

'CPD course,' he groaned. 'Basil reminded me the other day that I only have 4 points so I have to cram in the remaining 8 this month. It means I'm going to be spending my evenings learning about the law!'

'Ugh the law! I wonder could I learn a foreign language and use the hours as CPD points. I seem to have hardly any English clients anymore so it would be put to good use at work,' I quipped.

'Ha! Try running that one past the Legal Services Commission. Anyways I better dash. I'm really late as it is. Are you around tomorrow?'

'Not sure yet. I have to check with Basil.'

Basil controlled the office diary as though it was a military operation. He spent his days pouring over it, eating biscuits and getting fatter. I couldn't remember the last time he had appeared in court to represent a client. As a result he had no idea of the delays that we had to deal with now. To say that he was stuck in the 'good ol days' was an understatement.

'Enjoy,' I shouted after him as I pushed through the big heavy black doors.

On the way to my office I passed through reception and picked up the post from my cubby hole. As usual there was a big pile of envelopes and memos awaiting my attention. I scooped it under my left arm and trudged up the stairs, hauling the wheelie behind me. Once I had taken off my coat and kicked off my shoes I collapsed into my chair. At least the room had character I thought and when I was there late in the evenings it was almost cosy, especially in dim lighting.

My stomach grumbled. I was always starving after a day in court. I pulled open my top desk drawer hoping that some exciting snacks might have magically appeared while I was out but a squashed looking granola bar lay wedged between some paperclips and elastic bands. I decided to make some tea to have with it and then I would get stuck into the mound of post.

When I was nicely settled, I almost felt relaxed as I leafed through some memos that lay on top. Most of them were from the Crown Prosecution Services. I then got to a handwritten letter. Strange, I thought. I took a sip from the hot mug and sighed with contentment. There was something so comforting about a mug of tea. The letter was written in an untidy scrawl on a white A4 page. It wasn't unusual to get a handwritten letter from a client who was in prison but these were always written on the standard white and blue prison paper. It was odd to get a letter from a client who wasn't in custody.

I checked who it was signed from and it just read Shane. I wracked my brain for a client of that name. I started to read it. It was brief and I almost smiled when I had finished it. As I had read through it, it dawned on me who the Shane was. He was a client of mine from about 2 years ago who had received a four year custodial sentence for a domestic burglary. He was out now and it seemed he had decided to write to me to tell me this.

Shane had developed a crush on me and the office used to joke that the letters he sent to me from prison

49

were love letters. It got to the point where he made repeated friend requests on Facebook and I had to block him. I hadn't heard from him in a few months and I had presumed that he had forgotten about the whole thing. Obviously not I decided.

Throwing the letter in the bin I returned to the more important post. I spent about an hour sorting through what needed to be done urgently and what could wait until tomorrow. At 7.30 I wasn't even close to being finished but I decided that I couldn't take anymore so put on my coat, slipped my feet into my ballet flats and headed out of my office.

Before leaving the building I had a quick look at the diary in Basil's room, to check what I would be doing tomorrow. I could see that I was going to be in the office in the morning and that I was scheduled to attend Charing Cross Police station in the afternoon for a Voluntary attendance. This was someone who the police wanted to question but instead of arresting the person and taking them down to the station they made an appointment with the person to attend the station so as they could be interviewed. It was far more civilised and usually used by the police when a person didn't have any previous convictions or they felt that they weren't a flight risk.

CHAPTER NINE

As I pushed the door to our house open I could tell that Laura was home already. It warmed the heart to come home to the lights and heating turned on. In the sitting room she had some candles lighting and there was a bottle of red wine open already.

'Oh great, you're home. The takeaway should be here in about 20 minutes,' Laura said walking into the room, holding a wine glass in her right hand.

'That is music to my ears,' I said. 'I'm exhausted. How was your day?'

'Same shit different day. I ordered the usual by the way,' she said, quickly changing the subject. Like me, she rarely liked to talk about work once she had left her office. There almost seemed to be an unspoken mutual agreement that once we stepped into our house we left work outside.

'Have I told you how amazing you are?' I joked. 'Maybe if neither of us finds a man we should just get married! You can be the bread-winner and I'll be the hausfrau!' Laura smiled and poured a glass of wine for me.

'I'm just going to get out of this suit. I'll be down in a minute,' I called as I headed up the stairs.

I was just into my comfy leggings when I heard the doorbell ring. When I walked back into the sitting room Laura was already dishing out the food onto plates and she even had my favourite chutney on the table.

I grabbed a piece of naan bread and devoured it. 'I wish I could eat like you do and stay as thin as you,' Laura sighed.

'Eh Hello! You are so skinnier than me. Don't you realise it's going to be a struggle for me to get into your party dress from last year! Anyway enough of this stupid talk. Let's get stuck in. I'm absolutely starving.'

About two hours later while we were polishing off the wine and I was contemplating going to bed, Laura broke the easy silence.

'I'm thinking about quitting my job,' she stated as though she had just said that she was thinking of popping out to get a newspaper. I knew Laura really disliked her job but I hadn't realised it had reached this level.

'Why?' I exclaimed, trying not to be dramatic. 'I mean, I suppose I know why but...seriously?'

'I just don't know if I can take it any more Kate,' she said quietly. I don't have a life. The office *is* my life. How sad is that? I feel like I work, sleep a little and eat. Even when I'm not there I'm getting emails about what I need to be doing so I never really get to switch off. I knew the hours were going to be long before I got into it, but I had no idea that I would feel as though my life belonged to someone else.'

'Wow Laura, I really hadn't realised that you had reached this point with it.'

'For ages I thought I was just having a 'bad week', but now all the weeks are 'bad'. I feel like I hate my life. We're always promised a promotion. They're dangled in front of us like a carrot. But I've been passed over twice now. I really just don't know what I'm doing it all for. I know the money is good but as it stands I just don't have the time to even spend it.'

'I'll help you out there,' I joked, hoping to raise a smile from her. I was rewarded with a glimmer of one. Well at the very least her lips twitched.

'I don't know, maybe I'm just exhausted.'

'Why don't you take a holiday?' I suggested. I knew that Laura still had almost all her holiday days left to take, despite it almost being the end of the year. There seemed to be a feeling within her office that taking a holiday was a weakness and moreover I think the staff worried about the security of their jobs, particularly in these tough times.

'Do you think?' she almost whispered. I had never seen Laura looking so lost. She was usually so upbeat and positive. Her eyes were wide and she was fidgeting with her fingers.

'Definitely,' I stated. I hoped I sounded convincing. Laura needed someone to hold her by the hand for a little while. I hated seeing her like this.

Moving along the couch I engulfed her in a bear hug.

'Ugh!' she exclaimed. I hate that perfume you wear!'

This was more like the Laura I knew and loved. I decided to keep with the positivity now that I had her some way back to her usual self.

'What you need is a holiday in the sun. Seriously it would be fabulous for you. You just need to detox from London life for a while.' I was secretly quite proud of this statement. It almost seemed like a headline in a magazine. Hmm, I wondered if maybe there was a future for me in magazine journalism. Before my mind drifted too much I brought myself back to our living room. Focus Kate, Focus.

'Look why don't you head to bed. Then tomorrow go to your HR department and request 10 days off work and book yourself a holiday. If you still feel the same way after a break then maybe you need to consider a change of direction but I really think you should try the holiday option first.'

Suddenly I felt like my mother was talking. When had I become so reasonable? Maybe it was because I had spent the last three years at work helping other people sort out their problems?

'Thanks Kate,' Laura whispered. 'You really are the

best. I hadn't even thought of that as an option. Maybe I am just a little burnt out. I'm kind of scared to request the days off though. You know what they're like in there. Most of them think that a world outside the office doesn't exist.'

'I know Laura,' but in the long run it'll be the best thing for you. I hate seeing you like this. It doesn't even seem like I'm talking to my best friend. I think you probably *are* exhausted and your body is just crying out for a rest.'

'Come on. Upstairs to bed,' I ordered. 'I'll clear away the takeaway stuff and the glasses.'

'Do you ever feel like this Kate?' Laura asked, turning to face me before she headed up the stairs.

The truthful answer was that recently I was feeling resentful, angry and sad at where I had found myself. My career was nothing like I had imagined it to be. I had a student loan which never seemed to diminish, I struggled to pay the rent and of late I was really worried about my future. In the world of criminal defence, there was a standard rate that Lawyers like myself were paid. I had reached this and couldn't see any way of increasing it. This lack of an opportunity to progress was *so* frustrating. I wasn't the only one feeling this way. More often than not conversation in the advocate's room in London's various courts revolved around the pay cuts and the 'joke' that soon we would be working for free. Now wasn't the time to say this to Laura though.

'On and off,' I said vaguely as I headed into the kitchen. 'Sweet dreams.'

That night I tossed and turned, unable to fall asleep. The way Laura had described feeling today was exactly how I felt a lot of the time. I felt like I had almost wasted my life on exams and studying. Sure I had loved the University life but I had never really taken the time to step off the 'law-train' and see if I was actually heading in the right direction. The past few months had been a bit of an eye-opener for me. Until a couple of years ago, my friends and I had been more or less in the same financial position. However more and more of them were able to live a lifestyle that I couldn't and didn't see myself ever being able to afford. I found this so frustrating. Particularly when the majority of people presumed that as a lawyer I must be rolling in cash. Sadly this wasn't true.

I also felt scared. I could just get by now but I didn't have any savings and as for a pension on my current earnings I couldn't ever foresee myself being able to put money aside for one.

Cripes I really was throwing a pity party for myself. I looked at the clock. 5am. I started to count backwards from a hundred, hoping that I'd be lulled into a sleep. When the alarm sounded about an hour and a half later I felt as though I'd just fallen asleep. Dragging myself out of bed I toyed with the idea of calling in sick. My office gave us five paid sick days a year. I had already used two of them up so I supposed I should really keep the other three in case I really was struck down with something.

CHAPTER TEN

Later that day I walked into Charing Cross Police Station, cursing the rain. My feet were soaked. Ballet flats were no one's friend in the rain. I checked the time and realised I was ten minutes late. Hopefully that meant that my client, Mr. Galvin, would be here already.

I scanned the reception area of the police station. The chairs were filled with a right mixture of people. There were two elderly ladies, clutching their bags as though the teenager beside them was about to grab them and run. Although this probably wasn't beyond the realms of possibility. There were a couple of drug addicts, looking drawn and gaunt. In the corner sitting calmly in an overcoat was who I presumed to be Mr. Galvin. I walked towards the man who appeared really out of his comfort zone. His shoes were shined, his hair groomed and he was well washed. This might sound like a normal requirement for a person but considering the people I came into contact with everyday this attention to personal hygiene was very much appreciated.

'Mr. Galvin?' I questioned, walking towards him.

'Hello, you must be Miss Hunter. Pleased to meet you,' he said extending his hand. His sweaty palm gave away how nervous he was.

'Mr. Galvin, I understand that this is your first time being interviewed by the police about something. Is that correct?'

'Yes, Miss Hunter and......'

'Please call me Kate,' I interjected.

'Oh okay....well..em ..Kate I really don't know what to do. I mean I've never been in trouble with the police before...and now this..,' he trailed off.

I knew from speaking to Basil about Mr. Galvin, that the police intended to question him today about an allegation of a rape.

'Okay Mr. Galvin,' I said sounding brisk.

Usually someone in this predicament didn't want a female solicitor dealing with their case. It usually helped if I appeared not bothered by the subject matter. I knew that later I would have to assure him that in order for me to advise him properly he had to trust me completely and tell me the truth.

'What will happen now is that I'll phone the Officer dealing with this allegation. He will bring us through to the custody suite.'

Mr. Galvin looked panicked and the colour drained from his face.

'This is where the interview will take place as they don't have any interview rooms out here. You have attended voluntarily and from speaking with the officer earlier today, I know that he doesn't have any plans to arrest you.'

Mr. Galvin looked ashen now. It almost seemed as though the gravity of the situation had hit him at the mention of the custody suite.

I spoke with the Officer on my phone and he said that he would be out to get us in a few minutes. Mr. Galvin shuffled uncomfortably from side to side.

'It's awfully cold isn't it?' he said making nervous chit-chat. The poor man was completely out of his comfort zone.

'Yes it's freezing outside,' I said sympathetically. He was clinging to the normality of discussing the weather when he felt anything but normal.

Officer Leadberry appeared and I asked if Mr. Galvin could stay in the reception area while I received disclosure from him. I felt that he would be more comfortable out here as he was looking paler by the minute. Before heading into a consultation room with the officer I assured Mr. Galvin that once the officer had told me the details of the allegation, I would speak with him at length about everything. He sat down shakily.

'Right Miss Hunter, so how much do you know about this allegation at the moment?'

'Not a whole lot really, other than it's an allegation of rape by a 14 year old girl and that Mr. Galvin is 58.'

OIC Leadberry opened a thick folder and slowly shuffled around some papers. He coughed. 'Well for starters it's more than one allegation of rape. The 14 year old girl said he did it at least five times.'

Leadberry handed me a sheet of typed disclosure.

I read carefully through it. Rape cases were always difficult and sensitive matters for all involved.

'I intend to interview your client today about an allegation of rape made by a 14 year old girl. She alleges that he raped her at least 5 times. The complainant is someone who was doing work-experience at Mr. Galvins office. Her school has a 2 week work placement scheduled into their timetable and she was shadowing Mr. Galvin who is an accountant. The girl states that she was a virgin until this happened.

She has done an ABE interview to provide her statement.

This meant that she had been interviewed by two police officers and that this had been recorded by cameras. The reasoning for this was because of her age.

This is all that was written on the sheet. I went on to ask for further information.

'So when are these rapes alleged to have happened and can you give me more detail about each individual occasion?'

'About two months ago. The first time was when

she was there after office hours as Mr. Galvin had told her he would give her an insight into the various different types of accounts. The second time was in their office kitchen. The third time was in his office and the fourth and fifth times happened in the room which they had placed her to work from.'

'Why didn't she report it after the first occasion?' I questioned

'I don't think that really matters Miss Hunter, do you?' Leadberry said snidely.

'It's a perfectly legitimate question,' I stated calmly. 'Why didn't she report it after the first time?' I pressed.

'That's all I'm willing to disclose at this stage,' Leadberry said, closing his file. He was obviously pissed off. Tough, I thought. I wasn't here to be his friend.

I decided that I might as well press on. 'So has this girl made any previous reports of a similar nature to the police before?'

'That is all I'm willing to disclose Miss Hunter,' he said tersely.

'I will need more information about each individual time that she alleges he raped her.' I stated matter of factly.

'You know I'm not required to give you all the information available to me Miss Hunter.'

'Well, will you at least tell me her name then?'

'Rebecca,' he said as he opened the door to the consultation room for me, clearly indicating that he wasn't going to give any more information out at this point.

'Well shall we bring Mr. Galvin through?' I asked choosing to ignore his obvious bad mood. As we were walking back to the reception area I heard my phone ring. I decided to ignore it as Mr. Galvin was already on his feet, his hands clenched in front of him.

'Mr. Galvin, I'm ready to have a private consultation with you. If you'd like to follow me?'

He looked like he would prefer to take his chances and bolt through the sliding doors. However, my impression of him so far was that he usually did the right thing and in this instance it meant following me through the door to a place which he was terrified of.

As we settled ourselves into a consultation room, I explained to him that my advice was free, independent from the police and that it was covered by attorney client privilege. He clutched the Styrofoam cup of revolting smelling coffee which he had been handed by Leadberry. Initially he had looked highly suspicious when he had been asked if he would like coffee or tea. I think he suspected that the Met police would put some sort of drug into it which would make him sign a confession.

'Mr. Galvin,' I began.

'Please, call me Ted,' he said forlornly.

This made his hunched over figure seem even more vulnerable. I hadn't decided yet whether he was just a very good actor or if he was genuinely terrified about the allegation made against him.

'Right, Ted, let's just get some basics out of the way.'

I noted down that he was 58, married for 30 years and had three children aged twenty-six, twenty-three and eighteen. He worked as an accountant in a firm where he was a partner.

'Does your wife know about all this?' I queried.

'No, she has no idea. I can't tell her-it would just destroy her,' he said quietly.

'Ted, you know why you're here.'

I decided that it was time to stop avoiding the elephant in the room. He would have to face the issue, whether he wanted to or not.

'The Police have received an allegation from a 14 year old girl, that you raped her on five separate occasions,' I paused for a moment.

'I know that it may be an uncomfortable subject for you to talk about but I need you to be open and frank with me. Believe me, I'm on your side and I want to advise you so your interests are properly represented. Please don't be embarrassed about anything. I'm used to dealing with sensitive issues.' I hoped that this little talk would encourage him to talk honestly to me.

Ted had his chin on his chest and was staring at his shoes.

I decided to continue talking. 'Officer Leadberry has told me that the girl in question was doing a two week work experience placement at your firm and that on five occasions she was raped within the office. He hasn't given me any more information so really, now I need to get your side of the story.'

Ted didn't say anything for a few moments. He looked like he was trying to gather the strength to explain his side of the story. Eventually he spoke.

'It's all lies. All of it. I never even touched her inappropriately, let alone raped her,' he shuddered.

Something in his tone of voice made me believe him. I had yet to come across a man who admitted to a rape. No-one wanted to be seen as a sexual predator. Particularly because of the hard-time they would get if they went inside. I hadn't expected Mr. Galvin to admit to raping the girl but, there was something in his eyes which made me want to fight for him.

'Okay it's probably best to start from the beginning,' I said, my pen poised over my notebook ready to take notes as he was speaking.

'Well, the part about her doing work-experience at my office is correct. Our firm has an agreement with her school. We take three different students for a two week placement at various times during the school year. If I remember correctly she was at our office in September for two weeks.'

I furiously noted all this down.

'If the truth is told, I'm generally too busy to spend a lot of time with them, so it's generally the trainee accountants at our firm who show them a little of how the accounting world functions.'

He seemed a little calmer now that he had started talking.

'This girl, Rebecca, at least I think that was her name, seemed really enthusiastic which to be honest was a welcome surprise. Most of the work experience students we get, spend their time trying to get out of the office early and moaning about the photocopying we ask them to do. She asked if she could spend some time shadowing me and I couldn't see any reason for her not to.'

'Did you know this girl before she began the work placement?' I asked.

'No, I'd never met her before. As I said, we have an agreement with her school and we are never told who we're getting or whether it's a boy or girl. We just find that out when they turn up on their first day.'

'Did she ask you personally if she could shadow you?'

'Yes, she did. If I remember correctly it was a few days into her placement, which would make it a Wednesday. I was a bit harried at the time, as we were having a bit of a problem with a client of ours. I allowed her to sit in on a meeting with us.'

'How did she appear when she approached you?'

'She seemed like a particularly ambitious, go-get-em sort of kid.'

'Were you alone with her at all? Or even alone with her a lot?'

'Well what happened is this.' Ted appeared a bit more comfortable now and was sitting upright. He looked me in the eye, for the first time.

'I know I should have reported it to her school but I really didn't want to get her into trouble.'

'Reported what?' I asked gently.

'Well, I found that for the next few days she was extremely eager. She was constantly bringing me coffee, doing photocopying for me. She even offered to stay late to help me with some urgent work.'

'Did you think that there was anything strange about this?'

'Well, as I said I did think that it was unusual for a 14 year old to be so motivated but, I just saw it as almost refreshing. It kind of restored my faith in teenagers, to tell you the truth. Although I know that must make me sound like a doddering old man,' he said with a hint of a smile.

He sat quietly for a moment, seemingly deep in thought. I decided not to interrupt him as he appeared to have developed his own pace for telling me about events.

'Then on her second last day at our office she offered to stay late again to help sort a large amount of paperwork. That's when it happened,' he trailed off.

After a few moments I asked the all important question. 'What happened?' I asked softly.

'She came to me, and asked me for money,' he stated simply, almost as though it was the most obvious response in the world. I had not been expecting this reply.

'She said that she was pregnant and that she needed an abortion. She said her parents would go crazy. I think the words she used were that they would 'kill her.'

Now the words were rolling from his mouth.

'She seemed vulnerable and scared and I asked her to sit down. She almost collapsed into the chair opposite me. Then she started sobbing. I just didn't know what to do. I mean she was only fourteen. I handed her some tissues and waited for her to calm down.'

Mr. Galvin paused there but I didn't feel the need to prod him. He seemed lost in the memory of that evening at his office. After a sombre pause he began speaking again.

'Then when she seemed a bit more in control again I started asking her questions, such as whether anyone else knew and moreover why she had come to me for help, especially as she hardly knew me. She said that her boyfriend was the father of the baby and that he didn't know she was pregnant and neither did her parents. When I asked if she had seen a doctor or the counsellor at her school she began to get angry.

Then she asked if I was going to help her or not.'

I let Ted speak on, scribbling down everything he was saying.

'I felt really sorry for her. Honestly my heart went out to her but I knew that it wasn't my place to give her money. She needed real help and someone who could explain her options to her.

I told her this and said that I could speak to her school councillor if she felt this might help. When I said this, she stood up and her eyes were blazing. I remember clearly what she said next: if you don't help me you'll regret it. She stared at me coldly and then turned and walked out of the room. She didn't turn up for her last day at work.

The whole episode really shook me up, but I didn't tell anyone about it, even my wife. I knew I should probably have told her school, but I felt that she seemed to have enough problems without me possibly making it worse. That was the last time I saw her. Then two weeks ago Officer Leadberry contacted me to say that she had made an allegation of rape against me and that he wanted to interview me about it.

I swear, I haven't slept a full night since. My wife probably thinks I'm having an affair or something as I've been so preoccupied but I felt that I couldn't tell her. I'm hoping that it will all just go away after today. After I explain what really happened.' He looked at me expectantly.

I certainly hadn't been anticipating that and I hoped my face was neutral.

'She says she was a virgin until she met you. Did she mention anything about this to you?' I asked.

'No, as I said, she told me that she had a boyfriend who had gotten her pregnant. I would assume from this that she wasn't a virgin.'

'Is there anything else that you feel is relevant that you haven't told me Ted?'

'No, nothing that I can think of. What happens now? Will I be interviewed straight away?' The calm he had found while talking to me appeared to have disappeared and his face was once again taking on a panicked look.

I began by explaining his interview options to him. I told him that he could give a full and frank account to the police, just as he had done with me. I then explained that he had the option of doing a prepared statement. I explained to him, that if he decided to take this option, we would write out his version of events before the interview and that he would sign this sheet. I would then read this out at the beginning of the interview. The officers would proceed to ask him questions, as though I hadn't read out the statement, but that he could then answer all their questions with 'no comment'. Finally I explained that he could decide to exercise his right to silence and not answer any police questions.

Mr. Galvin looked terrified and I could almost see his neck muscles tense up.

'What do you advise me to do Miss?'

'Well Mr. Galvin, it appears to me that you have nothing to hide. My advice would be to put forward your story at the first opportunity. If you decide to go 'no comment', the police may think that you have something to hide. Also I feel that you would find a 'no comment' interview difficult to cope with.'

I didn't mean this as an insult to Mr. Galvin, but as someone who appeared to be used to telling the truth, I felt that he would be unable to not answer the questions which the police would be pummelling him with.

'All you have to do Ted,' I said gently 'is answer the police questions honestly and frankly. Speak to them just as you spoke to me. Also if at any point you want to stop the interview to speak to me that is perfectly okay. The tapes will be turned off, the officers will leave the room and we can have a further consultation.'

He seemed happy with this thought.

'Are you ready to do your interview then?'

He nodded.

I rose, and went to inform the officers that we were ready for interview. Any colour that had been in Mr. Galvin's cheeks had now left. He looked nervous and on edge.

Four hours after entering Charing Cross station, I walked through the sliding doors, leaving the stale air of the station behind me. I gasped as the cold air hit me. I felt drained. I hadn't had lunch and it was now approaching six o' clock. I decided against going back to the office at this hour. I wouldn't have been productive anyway as my brain was fried. I took out my phone and sent off a quick text to Basil:

Finished at Charing X-see you in the morning. I'll text you Mr. Glavin's result when I know it

Basil was one of those control-freaks who had a need to be in the loop at all times. I had battled against this when I had first started working at HBW but I had only ended up making life difficult for myself. It was far easier to do things as Basil wanted them done.

As I walked towards the tube station, I answered an incoming call from a 'blocked' number. I couldn't hear anyone at the other end. These calls with no one speaking at the other end were becoming a little strange.

'Hello? Hello?' I repeated. Surely it couldn't be a sales person as they were always eager to get their spiel in before they were hung up on. I decided to stop answering calls from 'blocked' numbers. If someone needed to leave a message they could do so.

CHAPTER ELEVEN

The rest of the week had passed in a blur and finally it was Friday evening. An entire two, work-free days stretched out gloriously before me. The 'Friday feeling' really was the best thing about working! Laura and I were heading out tonight to celebrate her bravery in asking for *and* getting 10 days off. It had taken her two days and a pep talk from me but she had gotten there. She had promised that the drinks were on her because until I was paid on Monday I was officially broke.

At least HBW were good about paying us on time. Some of my friends in other criminal defence firms could never be guaranteed if they were going to get paid on time. I knew from personal experience how unsettling it was to anxiously, check your balance on pay-day to find that you hadn't in fact been paid. My blood still boiled every time I thought about it.

Laura's off-key singing, shook me out of my reverie. How someone so petite could howl so much while in the shower never failed to surprise me. Although it was great to hear her in such a good mood. I had been really worried about her at the start of the week. The thought of ten days away from work seemed to have lifted a weight from her shoulders and she almost seemed like the Laura I knew from university, before she had begun working in the city. I wondered had I changed since I started working?

My deep thinking was interrupted by Laura barging into my room with a glass of something in one hand and a dress in her other. She shoved the glass into my hand.

'G&T. Enjoy,' she said, clinking her glass with mine. 'So what do you think of this dress?' she asked doing a little twirl. Does it hint that I work in a boring

68

office all day or does it suggest that I lead a fun and fabulous life?'

'Definitely the second one,' I replied while applying a second coat of mascara.

The dress *was* fabulous. It was a black elegant fitted with a low scooped back.

'You look sophisticated but fabulous. Okay,' I said glancing at the time on my phone. We have 20 minutes to fabulize ourselves before the cab arrives.'

'Did you just make up a word?' Laura smiled.

'Nope, I'm sure E TV have laid claim to it already,' I joked. 'Right we really better get a move on!'

Knocking back my drink, I stared at the two dress options I had laid out on my bed. I went for the midnight blue Reiss dress that Laura had tired of last year. Luckily we were both the same size. She really was a great friend I mused. I slipped on the dress and wiggled my feet into my heels. On second thoughts I decided I would pad around barefooted until the cab arrived. I knew that in a few hours my feet would be pinched in pain and I wanted to prolong this for as long as possible. I took a critical look at myself in the mirror. I had earlier curled my dark brown hair and it was just the way I liked it right now. It fell in loose waves around my shoulders but I knew by the time I got home it would probably be pancake flat. I had yet to master the art of getting curls to last all night. The blue dress was probably supposed to reach to the knee but because of my long legs it stopped well above that. Apart from the circles under my eyes, I felt happy with what I saw.

I checked that my handbag had the essentials in it, picked up my heels and headed downstairs to have another quick drink. I was *so* excited about tonight. It had been ages since I had had a night out with Laura.

Hearing the beep of the cab I yelled for Laura to

hurry up. I could feel the G&T's hitting me and I felt a wave of excitement. A girls night out really couldn't be beaten!

The following morning I lay in bed, wishing that the pain would stop. My head was pounding, my eyes were sore and my body felt as though it didn't have a drop of water left in it. Damn jagermeisters, I thought. We had met some of Laura's friends in the club and they had insisted on doing rounds of shots. Although I doubted I had put up much resistance at the time. I hauled myself into a sitting position, groaning with the effort and my eyes panned around the room for any signs of water. My dress from last night had been carelessly thrown on the floor and for some reason the contents of my handbag were scattered on my bed. No sign of water however. I was going to have to make the journey to the kitchen, which in my current state seemed like the toughest task imaginable. I sat still for a few more minutes to allow the spinning in my head to subside. Finally when I thought that I might actually die if I didn't get some hydration, I gingerly swung my legs over the side of the bed. Today was going to be one of those days where everything was going to be an effort.

As I passed Laura's bedroom door I could hear loud snoring. Obviously still asleep then I thought. In the kitchen I guzzled water as though I may never see running water again. I searched in vain for some painkillers. All I found were empty packets of Nurofen in the cupboard. I contemplated making something to eat for myself but decided that this would probably be too much of an assault on my body at this point. Refilling my glass with water, I headed back to bed for sleep in the hope that when I woke up some of the hangover would have eased.

That evening Laura and I sat around in the living

room waiting for our takeaway. Copious amounts of liquids during the day seemed to have bought my body back to resembling how it felt, before I decided to drown my liver with alcohol. Between both of us we had pieced the night together. Laura couldn't remember getting home but I could remember waving idiotically at taxis trying to hail one for us. I think we had eventually stumbled through our door giggling and very drunk somewhere around 4.30 this morning. I couldn't remember some of the club but Laura assured me that I hadn't kissed any of her friends. For some reason I had a horrible feeling she was lying to me but maybe this was just paranoia due to my hangover. Hopefully!

'So have you decided where you are going to go on holiday?' I asked Laura. She had managed to get the first 10 days in December off, so she would have to decide soon.

'Not completely but I think I have a good idea about what I want to do. The reason I'm going is because I need to relax and de-stress so I was kind of thinking of a spa somewhere in Asia. I have some stuff I printed off the internet upstairs. A few days with treatments and sunbathing could be just what I need,' Laura said sighing contentedly.

'You seem really happy,' I observed, 'and a little hungover!' I added.

'I am, and I have you to thank for it,' she said looking at me over the rim of her teacup. 'If you hadn't made me see the light at the end of the tunnel my hangover might not be going so well!' she joked with a wink.

'Always happy to help a friend in need,' I smiled. 'So you only have two more weeks at work and then you're off. You better choose your spa quickly.'

The doorbell sounded loudly and I stood to answer the door. Two takeaways in a week probably weren't the best for me but a hangover deserved a special dispensation I reasoned, as I thanked the delivery man. I shivered against the cold air and headed back to the warmth of the sitting room, where Laura had laid out plates while I had been at the door.

'Get stuck in,' I exclaimed, laying the various boxes on the table.

'So,' Laura began, after the edge had been taken from our hunger. 'What's going on with you then? I feel like you've been picking up my pieces this week but I haven't asked you how you are.'

'I'm fine, you know, same ol, same ol.'

'How's work going?' Laura continued.

'Probably best not to talk about it with a hangover.' I joked.

'No, seriously, how's it going?' Laura pressed.

I had a feeling she wasn't going to let this one drop. 'Well, you know,' I hedged, 'nothing has really changed.'

'So can I take it that you are still really unhappy then?'

'Hey, do we really have to talk about work? It's hardly the most interesting of topics,' I hedged.

'You just don't seem like yourself lately,' Laura said 'and I've been so busy or have been a bad friend, whichever way you want to put it but I haven't asked you about it.'

I decided that some honesty couldn't hurt, especially since Laura had cheered up at the thought of her holiday. I felt that if I had a moan it may not tip her over the edge.

'Well,' I hesitated. I really wasn't used to opening up about myself. I was the one who spent my days listening to other people's problems and trying to come up with a solution to them.

'I guess,' I began slowly, 'that I'm just really

disillusioned with law and the way the career seems to be changing.'

Uh-oh. I could feel tears pricking my eyes and I paused to blink and hold them back. I never felt very comfortable exposing my emotions. 'I just never imagined that it would be like this.' I put my hands around my knees, hugging my legs to me. I always felt comforted in this position. Laura knew this too and on seeing it, she moved closer to me.

'You know it's okay to moan about it,' Laura said with real empathy. 'I mean look at my mini-melt down earlier this week!' I appreciated her attempt to lighten the mood and cracked a weak smile. 'Are you able to put your finger on particular things which are getting to you or is it just everything in general?' Laura asked.

'Well, I suppose, what really gets to me is that there's the whole uncertainty around the cuts that they're making to the legal aid system. I almost feel that I'm stuck in a job that I really don't particularly like and I'm scared that I can't do anything else. I suppose I'm a bit terrified that they will reduce our fees by so much that I won't be able to survive on what I'll earn.' I felt as though I was on a roll now.

'Then there's the fact that I thought I could make a difference when I got into this career. I was probably being an idealistic student but I did genuinely think that I would be able to get innocent people acquitted. But I now know that this rarely happens. I seem to be processing people who are so used to the criminal system that they could probably represent themselves. I really did think that when I began working in this job that I would be able to help people who the system seemed to have forgotten about. I've realised that the most I can do is try and get the best result possible for someone at court and then I have to leave them go back to their lives.' I shook my head. I don't know why I find that so difficult to accept. I suppose I am helping them to some extent..' I trailed off and paused, realising that I had begun to sound as though I was ranting. I looked up from my fingers. I had been picking at the skin around my nails as I had been speaking, something that I always did when I felt agitated. Laura's eyes were wide and she really looked as though she didn't know how to respond. Sure I used to pass remarks here and there about how disgruntled I was with my job but I had never released so much information about it in one go.

'Wow,' was all Laura said at first. 'I didn't really know it was that bad. I mean, I knew that you didn't really like it at the moment but I just thought that it was a passing phase. You used to love it when you first started.'

'I know,' I said sadly.

This was definitely true. When I had started I thought that there was no better career. I wasn't stuck in an office constantly, which suited me and I used to find the work exciting. I could still remember the first time I had had to go and visit a client in prison. It had felt like I was in my dream job. I still did get a buzz from immersing myself in a difficult case and representing the client through it all to the end. It was probably one of the most satisfying feelings, when you knew that you had achieved the best possible result for a client. Maybe I had just lost sight of this and was getting caught up in all the talk among all the other advocates about the legal aid cuts. Perhaps I should focus on what I really enjoy about my job I mused and forget about all the other stuff.

'I have an idea,' Laura said her face brightening. 'What you need is a break from it all.'

'What I need is to win the Euromillions,' I said somewhat dreamily.

'No, I'm serious,' she said. 'Come with me on my holiday!'

She sat back in the chair, her eyes wide and a huge grin on her face, as though she had resolved the English debt crisis.

'Just one small problemo. As tantalizing as that sounds, I can just about afford to top up my oyster card at the moment. I don't think my budget would stretch to a flight to somewhere tropical!'

'No, of course not silly. I know that. That's why I'll be paying. Take it as your Christmas and Birthday present all in one.'

I stared at her gobsmacked. The difference in our bank balances hitting me squarely on the forehead. I hadn't been joking when I'd said that I could barely afford to top up my travel card and Laura had a spare few grand tucked away to throw at an exotic holiday. I didn't feel jealous though. I was well used to our differing finances.

'Honestly, you'd actually be the one doing me the favour. I'd much rather have someone with me when I'm falling over doing the down-ward dog and throwing back some health shot. Come on! It'd be amazing.'

She looked at me hopefully. She knew that while many of her friends would gladly take advantage of the invitation, I had difficulty accepting her generosity at times. It wasn't that I didn't appreciate her offer. It just made me feel a bit inadequate if the truth be told. Although, it would be amazing. My mind started to wander. I began to imagine sun and lying out without a care in the world.

'Well...?' Laura asked looking at me expectantly.

'You know I wouldn't be able to afford to pay you back at the moment. I could maybe do it in instalments when I have some spare cash. It would be amazing

Laura, but I'd feel really awkward accepting such a generous offer..' I trailed off as Laura butted in.

'I wouldn't offer if I didn't want you to come. It would make my holiday if you could come. *Please?'* she wheedled, giving me her puppy dog eyes, that I knew for a fact had always worked on her father when she was a child. They seemed to be having the same affect on me, as I could feel my pride dwindling.

'I'm in,' I said suddenly, almost before I had my mind made up.

'Yay!!!!' Laura said gleefully, clapping her hands in front of her. She threw herself on top of me, engulfing me in a bear hug. 'We're going to have *So much fun!'* she squealed.

'By the way,' I said grinning. 'Where exactly are we going?'

'My friend, you and I are heading to Bali for 9 nights! Well, as soon as you get the okay from frazzled Basil.'

'Ooh, how have I never called him frazzled Basil before? Yep I'm in the office tomorrow, so i'll make the holiday request first thing and I can text you when it's confirmed.'

I could feel my excitement levels rise and the misery I had been feeling a few minutes ago had dissolved. Maybe Laura was right. Maybe I needed to take my own advice and take a break from it all. Hopefully I might discover my zest for work after a holiday in Bali! What an emotional turn around.

I spontaneously hugged Laura. 'You know I really *really* appreciate this. You are an amazing friend.'

'I know, I know, I'm fabulous!' Laura laughed.

That night I fell asleep, mentally packing what I would bring. I hugged myself with excitement before drifting off into a peaceful sleep.

CHAPTER TWELVE

The following morning I practically floated into work. Even the crammed Northern line didn't dampen my spirits. Once I reached the office I went straight to my desk and booted up my aging computer. I was going to print out a holiday request form and put it on Basil's desk before I did anything else. Eyeing the mountain of post sitting on my desk, I decided to make myself a coffee while I waited for my computer to do its warm-up routine.

In the kitchen I bumped into Emily. When I say bumped into I actually mean it. The term kitchen was being extremely generous. It was more like a hamster cage with a kettle, some tea bags and occasionally a carton of milk could be found on the counter.

'Did you hear?' Emily almost gasped, clearly *dying* to disclose some juicy piece of information.

'Hear what?' I said turning towards her, my curiosity overriding my futile attempt at nonchalance.

Pleased that she had my attention, Emily basked in the knowledge that she knew something that I didn't. Emily was a very good case-worker but was as annoying as a fly which wouldn't stop landing on your leg.

Drawing a deep breath, she fixed her blonde ponytail as though she were on television. Obviously feeling adequately prepared she finally let it out.

'HBW are reducing the police station call-out fees,' she stated. She stood, surveying me, trying to gauge my reaction.

'What,' I spluttered. 'Reducing to what?'

'By twenty per cent on the first case at a station and then if you have a second case you will get half of what we used to get paid,' she stated dramatically.

Despite the fact that this should have affected Emily, in truth it didn't. She rarely did any out of hour's police station attendances. She was in the lucky position of living in an apartment in Chelsea which her father had bought her. The fact that she didn't have to pay rent meant that she was rarely found struggling out of bed in the early hours of the morning to attend a police station. I have to say I couldn't really blame her. If I was in the same position I probably wouldn't either.

'It's awful isn't it?' she said her blue eyes wide. I had to bite my lip to prevent some snide remark from slipping out. My good mood was rapidly evaporating and the dreams of sun and sand had disappeared.

'What?' was all I could muster. I was absolutely furious. 'But we haven't been consulted on this...,' I stalled, knowing that the partners really could do whatever they liked and didn't have to consult us on anything.

'And you've just signed over your duty slots to them for the next 6 months haven't you?' Emily said almost gleefully. She loved inflicting misery on someone else. Thankfully the kettle pinged to signal that it had taken a ridiculously long amount of time to boil the water.

'And they say a watched kettle never boils eh?' I said with fake cheeriness. I didn't want Emily to know that what she had said had really shaken me. 'Water?' I asked, holding the kettle above her pink mug.

'Yes please,' Emily said not moving her eyes from my face. She knew that I had had no idea that this was going to be implemented. For some unknown reason Emily and I had never got on and she seemed to take great joy in annoying me.

'Back to work for me then,' I said, hopefully sounding completely not bothered by what she had said. I chucked my spoon into the miniscule dishwasher and left to go back to my office. I sat down in my chair and took a deep breath. There was a growing ball of annoyance in my stomach.

Suddenly thoughts of my Dad's birthday present filled my head. If this was to take effect immediately I really would have to do an awful lot of out of hours work to be able to contribute to the gift.

Emily had been right when she said I had signed over my duty slots for the next 6 months to this firm. Duty slots were given to every solicitor who passed the exams to become 'duty qualified'. Every duty solicitor then signed over their slots to the firm they worked with, for a period of 6 months. Essentially HBW now had my slots for the next six months and without these slots I would find it practically impossible to secure a job with another firm. That is until the next round of slots were up in 6 months time.

Duty Solicitors received a rota covering a period of six months. Every court and police station will have a duty solicitor assigned to it at all operational times. So if someone were to be arrested and arrive at a police station without having their own solicitor they could request the services of the duty solicitor. The same was true for courts. If someone was charged to court and they arrived not having employed a solicitor, they could request to have the duty solicitor represent them. This service was free for the clients. The bonus for the firms was that, if a case didn't conclude at court on that particular day it may be possible to obtain a legal aid order to continue representing the client at any further hearings. This was additional income for the firm.

So essentially I was tied to HBW for the next six months and was powerless to do anything about the reduced rates they were now going to pay us for our out of hours work. To say I was irritated was an understatement. I had only signed over my slots to them a few weeks ago and they *must* have known that they were thinking of implementing cuts. It was *so* underhand of them to have acted this way. However I really couldn't do anything about it. It had always been my major gripe that while we studied for and had to pass exams to become duty qualified, once we signed the slots over to a firm, we essentially lost control of them. Grrrr!

I tossed the whole situation over in my head but really there was nothing I could do to change it. The thought suddenly occurred to me that maybe Emily had gotten the wrong end of the stick. It wouldn't be the first time I reasoned. I really should wait until it was officially announced I decided. Slightly cheered by this thought I began filling out the holiday request form. I could almost feel some of the tension leave my body, as thoughts of tropical beaches entered my head.

I gleefully signed my name at the end and fortified by the coffee, I walked towards Basil's office. From outside the door I could hear him on the phone and I paused for a moment to gauge his mood. He sounded like he was in typical Basil form. Moody, grumpy and generally in bad humour. I almost pitied whoever was on the other end of the line as Basil let loose a torrent of swear words. I stood debating with myself whether to just plough on and hand him the request form or whether I should try later, when he might be in a better mood. Although that could be quite a wait. In the three years I had worked at HBW I think I'd only ever seen Basil in a jovial mood at the Christmas parties and that was after he had drunk his body weight in whiskey.

Silence from behind the door told me that the conversation was over. I must have looked a right idiot standing there outside his door with my arm raised ready to knock, but frozen in place as I still hadn't made up my mind whether I should try later. Without any warning Basil stormed out of his office, colliding into me and causing me to stumble backwards against the wall.

'What the fuck?' Basil shouted. 'What the bloody hell were you doing standing outside my door like a bleeding statute?'

Crap, this really was an awful start to asking for holiday days. He was probably angrier now than he had been before he barrelled through the door. As I peeled myself off the floor and tried to stand up in a graceful manner, my eyes followed Basils to the ground. Lying there at my feet was my Holiday request form.

'Looking for a break eh? All getting too much for you is it?'

Crap, crap, crap, I thought. I bent to pick it up.

'Em, well, yes,' was all I could manage.

For some reason Basil sometimes terrified me and despite the fact that I faced Prosecutors, Judges and Magistrates in court everyday there was just something about him that made me lose the ability to act normal. Oh pull it together Kate, I chided myself. Taking a deep breath I handed the form to him. 'I'm requesting seven days off work at the start of December. If you could get back to me by the end of today I'd really appreciate it. An email would do,' I babbled. 'Thanks.'

Before I could humiliate myself further, I turned and almost ran down the hallway and into my office. Once there I sat down and took a deep breath. I glanced at the clock. It was only ten o' clock. What else did the day have in store for me, I wondered.

Later that day, I turned my attention to the pile of post which I had been ignoring all morning. How was it that I never seemed to reach the end? After ploughing through half of it, I came across a handwritten letter. It was short in the extreme, being only two lines long. My eyes flitted to the end where there was a scrawled signature-*Shane Reid*. God he's turning out to be needy I thought to myself. I read through it again and sat back in my chair. I had ignored his last letter and had passed it off as insecure Shane, who really didn't have anyone in his life who cared about him. This letter put a different slant on matters however. The last line read, *Why have you been ignoring my calls.*

All the calls I had been receiving from the blocked number now made sense. Several thoughts ran through my head. So it was clear that he was out of prison. He had told me as much in his earlier letter. But why did he want to contact me? Was he just trying to contact me as he genuinely believed I was his friends or was there something more sinister behind it? The numerous Facebook friend requests he had made lingered at the back of my mind. Initially he had emailed to contact me and then when I had ignored them he had made repeated friend requests. Eventually I had blocked him. I wondered was he annoyed about this. I knew that some lawyers, tried to keep clients onside by contacting them on Facebook or by text. Others sent 'gifts' to clients in prison. These usually took the form of cash. The idea really was to keep them sweet and also perhaps entice other prisoners to use them as lawyers. In the end it all came down to cash flow and the reality was that law firms were businesses out to make a profit. In these times with an increasing number of cuts being made, it was getting more and more difficult to make money from working as a criminal defence lawyer. I have had clients asking for money to get home, to use my mobile, drop them home from court, even pick them up from their homes and take them to court.

It had been standard practice in the past, when detainees were allowed to smoke at the station, for lawyers to hand out boxes of cigarettes to keep their clients nicotine habit in check but also to ensure that clients asked for them again when they were arrested. Who were you more likely to ask to represent you-the solicitor who gave you a continuous supply of cigarettes or the solicitor who was only interested in doing his or her job and providing advice but not the cigarettes?

As I was musing about this, Nick strolled into the room. He had two cups of steaming coffee in his hands.

'Nick have I told you before that I love you?'I joked. Coffee was just what I needed.

'You'll have to get in line Kate and it's a *very* long line,' he said with a grin. Nick was well aware of the affect he had on the ladies, but he seemed to find it all very humorous. He placed my mug in front of me. The coffee was made just as I like it, hot and strong.

'Sometimes I think that I'm addicted to this stuff,' I said as I sipped the hot liquid.

'Tell me about it,' Nick said. 'Herbal teas just don't have the same bang though do they? Anyway my reasoning is that it's a hell of a lot better than drinking during the day.'

Nick was probably referring to Stephen, a solicitor in our company who was well known for 'irishing' up his coffees in the afternoon. The funny thing was that he didn't really make any attempt to hide this little habit. In fact he often openly joked about how the job had driven him to it.

'What's this?' Nick asked, picking up Shane's letter. 'What the hell?' he exclaimed after reading it.

'What does he mean why haven't you been answering my calls? What's all this about Kate?'

'Honestly, I don't really know Nick. I mean, I told you all about the Facebook requests. Then I didn't hear anything from him for ages and out of the blue last week I had a letter from him which basically just told me that he was now out of prison. Then recently I've been getting phone calls from a blocked number. Initially I thought I was missing calls from the police station but then when no-one was leaving a message I decided not to answer any calls from a blocked number. Then this today,' I halted. 'I don't know whether I should be worried or not,' I added after a moment, taking another sip of my coffee.

I clutched the cup in my hands, warming them. Holding a mug like this seemed so comforting. Blurting all that out to Nick had suddenly made me feel worried.

'He was a strange one though wasn't he? Didn't really seem to have any idea of social boundaries,' Nick said in response. Although thinking about it that could be the majority of our clients,' he joked lightening the mood.

'That's for sure,' I said with a weak smile.

'You don't think I need to bring this to Basil's attention, do you?' I asked hesitantly. I couldn't think of anything I'd rather do less, especially after this morning's episode.

Nick seemed to be considering my question. His reaction to the letter was worrying me.

'I'm not sure Basil would do anything about it,' he replied eventually. 'I think he would see it as potentially losing a client, because we all know Shane will be back,' Nick smiled.

'He really will,' I said smiling back. Shane was the definition of a career criminal. It didn't matter what punishment or treatment programme the court suggested for him, eventually he would end up doing what he knew best-committing crime. It was probably just a matter of time before he was knocking at our door again.

'How about you just leave it for now and if he does try and get in contact again, let me know and we can decide what to do about it?'

I was reassured now that I had Nick on my side. He was right about Basil. Despite the alarming number of pay cuts, the partners were putting so much pressure on him to keep profits up. His attitude at the moment was to keep clients happy, almost regardless of any negative implications this may have.

'Seriously Kate, if you do hear from him again, promise you'll let me know? We don't exactly deal with the sanest of people at times so who knows what's going through his mind.'

'I will, and Nick, thanks for listening.'

'Anytime, anytime,' Nick said as he strolled towards his desk to answer the phone.

'Nick Cannon speaking.'

I was just about to drift into a daydream, when I noticed Nick shrugging on his coat and pulling his scarf around his neck. 'Where are you off to?' I questioned.

'That was the Defence Solicitors Call Centre. I'd actually forgotten I was on duty today. There's a male adult at Wandsworth Police station and they're ready for interview, so I'm out of here again. I really could have done with getting some paperwork out of the way,' he said eyeing the mountain of paper on his desk.

'I know, I've pretty much been at mine all day and it doesn't seem to have lowered at all,' I said dejectedly.

'Although you did get a little distracted by your love letter,' Nick said wryly. 'By the way, I'm on call until 11 tonight. Any chance you could back me up if I need help?'

'Sure, no problem.'

Nick, like Emily, rarely did any out of hours police station attendances. His father was something big in some big corporation and despite the fact that Nick was thirty-five, his father still paid him a very hefty monthly allowance.

As Nick grabbed his backpack and headed out the door I decided to check my emails. It was almost five o' clock and surely Basil would have emailed me his decision on my holidays by now. As I clicked into my inbox I almost held my breath. Basil really could play God with our lives.

My eyes scanned down the list of new emails. Bingo. Basil had emailed me at 3.10 this afternoon. How had I not seen this earlier? I anxiously clicked into it. Almost holding my breath I read through it.

Kate,

As you will be aware the time before Christmas is usually an extremely busy time for us, particularly with the increase in shoplifting. I have already granted two members of staff holiday leave for the same dates as you have requested. Unfortunately, for these reasons I'm going to have to refuse your request.

If you have any questions please do not hesitate to contact me.

Kind Regards,

Basil.

My heart sunk. Kind bloody regards my ass. The only question I had for him was why he was such a Grinch. I knew that the firm would be more than capable of coping without 3 members of staff for a few days, particularly when I was the only solicitor who had requested the time off. Ugh. I felt upset and angry. I picked up my phone and dialled Laura's number. As expected she didn't answer her phone and I didn't bother leaving her a message. I decided on a text instead.

Basil is officially the Grinch who stole Christmas. He has refused my holiday request☹

My phone told me it was 5.45pm. I couldn't do anymore work now and decided to call it quits. I shut down my computer and gathered my things together. As I was buttoning up my coat and wondering where I had thrown my scarf, the phone on my desk rang. I deliberated for about 6 rings whether or not to answer it. Sighing I reached for it and almost fell over as I attempted to grab my scarf from under my desk and say 'hello' in a normal voice.

'Kate, there's a Mr. Gatt on the line for you. Are you available to take the call?'

I wracked my brains to try and remember a Mr. Gatt. I dealt with so many clients on a daily basis that I found it very difficult to remember exactly who everyone was.

'Did he say what it was in connection with?' I asked, hoping for a nugget of information which would help me remember who he was. 'He says it's private.'

That old chestnut, I thought. For some reason certain clients felt that they couldn't disclose anything about their case to the receptionist, caseworkers, or anyone other than their solicitor. Nicks theory was that they liked to think that they were involved in some big scandal and that it gave their lives some excitement. I have to say I didn't disagree.

'Mr. Gatt, hello, how can I help you?' I asked, my voice certainly not portraying how upset I really was.

'Miss Hunter?' a deep voice intoned.

'Yes?' He had obviously clicked that I hadn't the foggiest idea who he was. 'I'm the accountant for HBW. I'm phoning regarding your out of hours invoices.'

'Oh?'

'It appears you made a mistake in two of your claims?'

Seriously could this day get any worse? I just wanted to crawl onto the sofa with a blanket and fall asleep. It was one of those days which just needed to be put to bed.

'I'm afraid I don't understand, Mr. Gatt.'

I had submitted 3 out of hours invoices for last month. I was counting on this money for Christmas presents.

'Miss Hunter, as you are aware, out of hours claims can only be claimed in full if you leave for the station after office hours, that is 6pm. However your claims show that on one occasion, you left the office at 5.56 and on the second occasion you left the office at 5.50. This means that you will only be paid half of the amount claimed for each of those but of course you will be paid the full amount for the third attendance. That is of course before tax.'

Suddenly it hit me that this was probably a hoax set up by Nick. 'Ha, Ha, very funny Nick. You almost had me!'

'I'm sorry, Miss Hunter?' a confused sounding voice said.

Crap, maybe it really was the accountant. Previously the firm had been lax about the 15 minutes from 5.45 and 6.00pm and would pay the full out of hours, if you left just a few minutes before official office closing time. It looked like this was no longer to be the case. Bloody recession, I thought.

'But I didn't receive any notice about this,' I stuttered.

'As you will be aware Miss. Hunter, it was always company policy to pay out of hours from 6pm. They were a little lax about this in the past but in light of current reductions in rates, the decision has been taken to enforce the rule strictly.' God he was such an accountant I thought.

'Ok, well, fine, thank you for letting me know,' I said wearily.

I hung up and almost laughed. I mean really, could this day get any worse. Actually I didn't even want to think of the possibilities. It seemed that anything could happen today.

I grabbed my bag and headed towards the door. I really just wanted to get out of the office without bumping into anyone else. I badly needed a couple of days away from it all and thank God it was Friday. As I stepped out into the cold late November air, I don't think I was ever as happy to leave the office.

CHAPTER THIRTEEN

That night, after spending a couple of hours watching reality TV I felt remarkably better. I had cheered myself up with the thought that it was almost Christmas and December in London was always fun. Who needed a 10 day holiday in Bali? Not me (I was still working on convincing myself of this)

Just as I was contemplating going to bed, my phone began to ring. Glancing at the screen I saw Nick's name. My heart sank. The only reason he would be phoning so late night was because he had someone at Wandsworth Police station for interview. I had completely forgotten that I had said I would back him up.

'Hi Nick,' I said wearily.

'Kate, hi!' I could hear music in the background so I presumed he was standing outside the door of a pub somewhere.

'Are you still okay to attend Wandsworth tonight? I have a youth in for GBH and they're ready for interview.'

Taking a deep breath, I gathered my composure. The last thing I wanted to do right now was finish off my Friday with a trip to Wandsworth. 'Sure Nick, that's no problem. Can you just text me through the details?'

'Yes absolutely. Kate you are a lifesaver!' he said with genuine enthusiasm.

'No worries and have a good night!' I said with a cheeriness I didn't feel.

After hanging up the phone, I sat on the sofa, willing myself to stand up. I felt absolutely shattered and a trip to Wandsworth seemed like it would require a monumental effort. Standing I walked wearily up the steps to my bedroom to change out of my comfy clothes. I pulled on my standard 'going to the police station in the night time' outfit. This consisted of jeans, boots, a warm jumper and a scarf. I knew some friends who, when woken in the middle of the night had pulled on a coat and uggs over their pyjamas and headed straight to the station. I would love to see a client's face on seeing their solicitor in their pyjamas with bed hair! I hadn't reached these levels yet but tonight I certainly felt close to it.

When I arrived at the station at about 11pm, the area was eerily quiet. I buzzed through to custody and sat waiting in the front office. About 15 minutes later, I was still waiting there. I decided to phone through again. I knew that this would only annoy the detention officers but frankly I was beyond caring at this point.

'Hello, this is Miss Hunter. I phoned through about 15 minutes ago. I'm in the front office and waiting for DC Rose.'

'Yes, we are aware that you are here. We're trying to contact DC Rose. When we do he will be with you when he's ready,' a curt voice said.

I swallowed a snide reply. It really irritated me when the officers told us that they were ready for interview and when we arrived, we were left waiting for long periods of time.

'Okay, I'll just continue waiting then,' I said probably sounding as curt as he had done.

I sat again, taking out my iphone and began to play Tetris. Oddly I found this game relaxing. Ten minutes later and nowhere near my top score, the door in front of me opened. A tall man with broad shoulders walked towards me, followed by a tiny lady. Well standing behind this giant, she almost seemed like a hobbit. They really were an odd duo. I wondered would they be playing good cop/bad cop during the interview.

'Miss Hunter?' the woman questioned, popping out from behind the DC who resembled either a bodyguard or a bodybuilder. Obviously I'm Miss Hunter, I thought to myself. I'm the only person here and I'd hardly be down here playing Tetris for giggles on a Friday night.

I plastered a smile on my face.

'Yes. I presume you are the Detectives dealing with Scott Ryan?'

'Yes, sorry about the wait. We were just trying to contact his father or mother to act as an appropriate adult. He's only 13 and it's his first time arrested so you can imagine that he's quite frightened. We've managed to contact his father and he should be here within an hour,' she said in a strong Geordie accent. She seemed to be the talker of the two.

My heart sank. Inevitably, this meant that he wouldn't arrive for well over an hour.

'Well how about we do disclosure while we're waiting?' I asked, trying to use the time efficiently. At this time of night, particularly on a Friday night the aim was to try and get in and get out of the station as quickly as possible.

'Yes, absolutely. I'm DC Rose and this is DC Faber,' she said gesturing towards the giant. He nodded which made me wonder if he talked at all or if he was employed solely to look intimidating.

'If you'd like to follow us?' the voice for both of them said, standing back against the door so as I could walk through. Cripes he was a giant. I was 5 10 and usually felt pretty on par with tall people but he towered above me.

I followed behind them as they guided me towards the custody suite. At the desk, it was a hive of activity. There were three people being booked in, all looking as though there were at varying degrees of drunkenness.

The phone was ringing but no-one was answering it. I stood in front of the custody sergeant waiting for him to notice me. After deciding that he was enjoying ignoring me, I coughed and waved my business card in his direction to get his attention. He had no option but to look up.

I smiled and asked for Scott's custody record.

'Sorry about the wait out there,' he said taking me by surprise. I hadn't been expecting him to apologise and it made me feel bad for being curt with him on the phone. 'We're just really backed up in here,' he said gesturing towards the chaos surrounding the desk as one of the drunk detainees began screaming and struggling with one of the detention officers.

'Hey, it happens,' I said giving him a genuine smile.

I turned towards the Detectives and indicated that I was ready to follow them towards the room where I would receive disclosure from them. I sat facing both of them. DC giant, as I had now started calling him in my head, looked extremely uncomfortable in the chair. He looked like an adult sat in a chair which is used in primary school.

DC Rose handed me a sheet of typed disclosure, which essentially outlined why the police believed Scott had been arrested. I read through it carefully.

'The victim, is a 21 year old female. She is currently in hospital, receiving treatment for her injuries. Photos will be shown.

She was on her way to Lidl this afternoon and took a shortcut down an alleyway. This was approximately 14.10. As she was walking she heard voices behind her and she quickened her step. She glanced behind her and saw 4 youths. She recognises one of them as Scott Ryan, as he lives 2 houses down from her and she is friends with his sister. Because of their demeanour she felt intimidated and started to walk more quickly. Suddenly she was hit from behind with an object. She fell to the floor. She was kicked repeatedly to the ribs and legs.

That is the last she can remember. She awoke in hospital.'

I digested this information, reading through it and formulating questions to ask Detectives.

'How did she end up in hospital?'

'A member of the public, who has provided a statement, was taking the same shortcut, on his way to Lidl when he came across her. She was completely unconscious and initially he feared she might be dead. He phoned for the police and an ambulance and waited with her until they arrived.'

'Did the victim recognise the other 3 youths?'

'No.'

'Would she be able to identify them again?' I pressed. I was surprised at how candid the Detectives were being with disclosure. Sometimes officers didn't like to give too much away and we went into consultation with our clients, aware that we didn't have the full story. Of course we pressed them for information but sometimes it was obvious that they had a trump card, which they couldn't wait to reveal at interview. It sometimes made advising clients difficult.

'They were wearing hoods and scarves wrapped high around their faces so she doesn't feel that she could.'

'What was Scott wearing?' I questioned, curious as to why he hadn't protected his identity as the others seemed to have done.

'Scott didn't have a hat or scarf on, which made it easy for her to recognise him.'

What *was* Scott playing at, I wondered. If he had

been intending on attacking someone, surely he would have taken the same precautions as his friends. Something just didn't seem to add up.

'Was anything taken from the vicim?'

'Yes, she had a handbag with her and that was taken. In it were her house keys, about £60 cash, her credit cards, blackberry and other personal items.'

'So will you be further arresting Scott for robbery?' I asked.

The giant, moved his head in what I assumed was a nod. I turned my head to the voice of the two and raised my eyebrows, waiting for a verbal answer.

'Yes.'

'Will you be carrying out forensics on the bag?'

Again a monosyllabic yes was the answer. I think she was getting tired of talking. I wondered whether the giant would take over the questioning at interview.

'Right, well I don't have any further questions. I'll speak with Scott now and when his father arrives you can direct him here. I don't want him left alone in his cell any longer.'

I imagined that he was pretty scared, as he hadn't been arrested before.

The detectives left the room and as I began filling out some paperwork I could feel my eyes beginning to droop. About ten minutes later, a small scared looking boy was lead into the room. I could see he was petrified. As the officer left him, he stood by the closed door, looking at me with wide eyes.

I smiled at him and introduced myself, explaining that I would be his lawyer at the station and that I was on his side. I motioned for him to sit in the chair opposite me. He looked somewhat relieved and as he sat in the chair opposite me I could see some of the tension ebb from his body. I started explaining that his father was on his way and his eyes widened. So far he hadn't uttered a word and his shoulders were hunched.

'Does he have to?' he asked in a tiny voice.

'I'm afraid so Scott. As you're only thirteen, the law requires that you have what's called an 'appropriate adult' present at your interview. The police have already contacted your father to act as your appropriate adult and apparently he's on his way. As soon as he arrives we'll have a long chat about why you are here and what happened in the alleyway this afternoon...,'I trailed off as I heard a commotion outside our door.

'He fucking wouldn't do any shit like that would he? He's my fucking son.'

I could see Scott visibly shrink into himself. Oh dear I thought to myself. This was going to be a long night.

The door opened and the giant led in a man who was half his size, black and looking extremely irate.

'Scott, what the fuck is all this about? I was fucking down the pub and I get a phone call from the police that you've been arrested. What the fucks going on?' He was quivering with anger. Although he stood a few feet away from where I was sitting I could smell the alcohol from his breath. There was no way I was going to allow this drunken man be present at Scott's interview.

I glanced over at Scott and could see that his father's presence at this interview was not going to be productive. He appeared frozen on the edge of the chair and looked as though he was trying to block out his surroundings. I stood.

'Why don't we all have a chat outside the room?' I said addressing the officers.

'Scott will you be ok in here on your own for a few minutes?'

Scott nodded, looking relieved at the possibility of not being in the same room as his father.

The two detectives, Scott's father and I walked outside. Standing in the hall I turned towards Mr. Ryan and introduced myself, wrongly presuming that he would be civil towards his son's lawyer.

'What the fuck am I down here for if he's got a lawyer. That's your job isn't it?' he said staring at me. His eyes were glassy, bloodshot and wide with anger.

It was obvious that no-one wanted Mr. Ryan to be present and he clearly didn't want to be here, despite his son being in custody. I decided to try the diplomatic route.

'Mr. Ryan, if you'd rather not be here, the police can arrange for someone from social services to act as an appropriate adult for your son. Would you rather that?' I looked hopefully at the detectives.

The giant was nodding enthusiastically. 'It would take about another hour but it wouldn't be a problem to organize, he said in a deep booming voice.

I had to prevent my mouth from gaping open. The giant speaks!

I turned towards Mr. Ryan. 'If you'd like to give me your telephone number I can phone you when we're finished with the interview and give you an update?'

'Don't bother,' he said already walking away from us.

I don't know where he thought he was going as he wouldn't be able to exit the building without the police. He must have realised this because he turned and almost yelled, 'Well is anyone goin' to let me out of this fuckin' building?'

DC Rose sighed and walked towards him. She looked like she wanted him ejected from the station as quickly as possible. I turned towards the giant.

'Can we try and get someone from social services here as quickly as possible then? I'm very conscious of Scott's age and that it's his first time in police custody.'

'Shouldn't be a problem.'

I stifled a yawn. 'I'll go speak with Scott then. I'll

buzz when I'm finished and hopefully the appropriate adult will have arrived by then.'

The giant opened the door to the consultation room and Scott sat upright in the chair, his hands clenched in front of him. He was wearing the obligatory baggy hoody and large jeans but his demeanour couldn't be further from the usual youths I met at the station. He seemed genuinely terrified.

I sat facing him once more.

'Miss, what's going on?' he asked quietly. I hadn't expected him to speak.

'Well Scott, your father needed to be somewhere else, so someone from social services is going to come and act as your appropriate adult. Remember I told you that this was necessary because of your age?'

He nodded.

'Let me explain what's going to happen from now on ok?' I said gently.

Looking relieved, he sat back in his chair.

'You've been arrested because the Police think that you used a brick to knock a lady unconscious.' I went on to explain what the Detectives had told me. He looked visibly shaken.

Just as I was about to ask him for his version of events there was a knock on the door. DC Giant popped his considerable bulk through the door.

'The appropriate adult has arrived. Turns out there was already one at the station for another matter and he is willing to stay on a little longer for this interview. Would you like him to join you for your consultation?'

I did a scream of joy in my head but kept this to myself. I might actually get home to bed at some point tonight.

'Yes please.'

From behind the giant emerged a pale thin man, probably about 22, dressed in red skinny jeans and a hoody.

He sauntered into the room and sat on the chair next to Scott. 'Anton' he said nodding in my direction. Did Anton have a surname I wondered? I handed a business card to him and updated him on where we were in the proceedings.

He obviously favoured head nodding above talking, as he nodded at me when I had finished. I turned to face Scott and asked him for his version of what had happened earlier this afternoon. I was struggling not to yawn, but Anton didn't even bother to try not to. I could see every one of his many fillings as he let us know how tired he was.

'Well Miss,' he began. At least he was polite I thought. 'You've seen my dad. He doesn' really care what I do innit, so I've been staying at friends houses for the last few weeks...' he stopped talking and began fidgeting with his fingers again.

'Go on Scott,' I said gently. 'If you want me to help you I need to know what happened from your point of view.'

'Well, the guys I've been with are all part of a gang innit. They told me that I could join but if I wanted to make it in I would have to do something to show that I'd be loyal to 'em. One of 'em came up with the idea of hitting a woman with a brick and robbing her.'

He stopped, clearly nervous. Even if I hadn't known before that Scott wasn't used to the legal system, what he had told me would have given me a clue. I believed what he had said. Also any kid who was part of a gang wouldn't tell me about the gang. That was the first rule of being a gang member. Scott was becoming very close to being a grass which could get him in all sorts of trouble with the gang leaders. He seemed to have spoken honestly, which didn't happen very often with youths. Sometimes they tried to develop some fantastical story which they thought might convince the police of their innocence. I suspected that Scott wasn't a fully fledged gang member.

He seemed reluctant to keep on talking so I nodded encouragingly at him.

'They made me do it. I didn't want to at first, but then they said that I wouldn't be able to roll with 'em if I didn't do it. I had nowhere to stay. I can't live with my dad 'cos he beats the shit out of me so I need to stay with the gang. I need some protection.'

'Did they threaten you with violence if you didn't do it?'

'Well, no they didn't say that, but I wouldn't have any protection. I'd be livin' on the streets. I was scared Miss.'

I sat back in my chair, considering everything that he had told me. I needed to decide what the best advice to give him for interview was.

'Why didn't you cover your face Scott?'

'They wouldn' let me. They said it was a true test of my loyalty to them.'

It sounded from what the police had said, that they felt certain he had been the one to throw the brick. If he was charged with GBH he may have a chance of running the defence of Duress, in which case it would be best to put forward his version at the earliest opportunity. I could feel my eyelids drooping, and shook my head slightly to keep awake. Although fear of violence would have been a lot easier to run at trial than fear of sleeping on the streets.

'Did you take the ladies bag?'

'No, the minute I threw the brick at her, I legged it. I was terrified. I didn't even see if she fell down Miss.'

I decided that the best thing for Scott to do was to put forward his story now and I went on to advise him on how the interview would work. Scott did really well in the interview. He answered the questions as best he could and when the interviewing officers had sealed the tapes and left he turned and looked at me with hopeful eyes.

'Did I do okay Miss?' he asked anxiously.

'You did really well Scott,' I said reassuringly.

'What happens now Miss? Will I have to go to court? Will I get out of here?' he asked sounding almost panicked.

'Scott what happens now is that the police make a decision based on what you said in your interview and also on the evidence they collected today. I feel that they will charge you to court but that you will be given bail tonight as you don't have any previous convictions.'

Scott absorbed this information before nodding in what I assumed was acceptance of the situation.

'Will you be there for me at court Miss?'

'Yes of course I will Scott. Do you have any other questions you want me to answer?'

He shook his head from side to side an stood silently, ready to go back to his cell until a decision was made.

CHAPTER FOURTEEN

Much later, probably at about 4am, I put the key in the front door of my house. I was absolutely shattered and couldn't wait to curl up under the duvet. Scott had been charged with GBH and very shortly after the interview he had been released on bail to attend Camberwell Green Youth Court in about a week's time. The police had given him a lift to his father's house and I had felt so sorry for him as he had fearfully climbed into the back of the car. But short of bringing him back to my house there hadn't been another address to bail him to. I crawled into bed and drifted off to sleep, grateful that today was Saturday morning and that I wouldn't have to get up in a couple of hours.

What seemed like a few moments after I'd fallen asleep, Laura bounded into my room with far too much energy.

'Come on sleepy head-it's almost two o clock. You are going to waste your whole weekend in bed. Were you out drinking last night?' she asked eyeing me suspiciously.

Deciding that any attempts at further sleep would be futile, I poked my head out from under the duvet.

'No, working,' I croaked.

Laura pulled a face. 'I can't believe fudging Basil refused your holiday request,' she said dramatically.

I smiled. 'Still keeping up with the fudging then. I know. I was seriously gutted. Yesterday was one of those days which just kept sucking the life from me.'

I hauled myself up into a sitting position. 'I've just accepted it now though. There's no point in moaning about it. My boss is an asshole. C'est la vie,' I shrugged.

'You know what you need? A run. How long is it

since you've actually put on your trainers? You used to do it almost every day and I can't remember the last time I saw you head out for a run.'

Laura was right. I used to run most days when I was training to be a lawyer. I'd even run a few marathons. But lately, work seemed to be sucking the life from me. I was constantly exhausted. I wasn't sure if I even knew where my trainers were anymore.

'Maybe today's the day,' I mused. 'Perhaps I'll go for a run today.'

'My work here is done,' Laura exclaimed as she headed out my bedroom door.

'Oh and don't forget we have leaving drinks tonight for Amy. Let's have a few sneaky ones here before we go. I have a bottle of prosecco that is just crying out to be drunk.'

Amy was a mutual friend who had just chucked in her job as a lawyer in the city and was heading travelling.

'Sounds great,' I said as I swung my legs over the side of the bed. Laura was right. Maybe I just needed to start doing the things I used to enjoy before work started to take over.

Later that evening I headed out the door for a run. I had located my trainers in the cupboard under the stairs buried under a pile of spare sheets. I started at a really slow pace and decided to go once around the common which was about 3 miles. A year ago I would have had no problem doing this. However, I was discovering that my lack of movement had really caught up on me. I could feel my legs burning and I felt out of breath after about a mile.

Cripes I thought. How did this happen? I resolved there and then that I was going to get my fitness back. Maybe even do a marathon next year I thought cheerily. Although maybe I'll just try and get around the park without having a coronary first. When I returned to our front door, I was completely out of breath, but I felt a sense of exhilaration as well. As hard as the run had been I had really enjoyed it. As I stood gasping for breath I thought about how I had allowed HBW to take over my life? More work life balance is what I need I thought. God these endorphins were making me Miss Motivation! I definitely needed a bit more of this in my life. Now I was really looking forward to going out tonight.

A few hours later, Laura threw a slinky top in my bedroom door.

'Here, take this. I've decided that it makes me look translucent. The silver and my blonde hair aren't working. It would look fabulous on you though with your dark hair.'

I gratefully took the top from Laura. I was always willing to accept her hand-me –downs. Especially as I hadn't decided what I was going to wear for the night. I pulled it on gently as she headed to the kitchen to top up our glasses. I looked in the mirror. It was perfect with my black skinny jeans. I loved how the back dipped, revealing quite a lot of skin. I turned, looking at myself from different angles, trying to decide what shoes would go with it.

'Whoa, check you out. You look hot!' Laura whistled. She handed me my glass, topped up with prosecco. The combination of the bubbles and the fact that it was the weekend was making me very excited about going out.

'Okay. Ben and Sarah are swinging by in a taxi in 20 minutes and we'll all head in together,' Laura called as she headed back to her room to do her makeup.

As I put on another coat of lipgloss, I had to shake

the niggling thought that it was quite sad how I really did live for the weekends. My weekdays seemed to be an endurance and come to think of it so did some of my weekends and evenings if I was on call. Come on Kate, don't think like that or you'll get all morose again. It's the weekend. With that, I could hear the taxi beeping outside and I banished all negative thoughts to the back of my head.

I threw back the rest of the Prosecco as I grabbed my handbag and checked for the essentials. Wallet, lipgloss and housekeys. As we clambered into the taxi Ben whistled. 'Check you two out! You both certainly scrub up well.'

'Thanks Ben,' Laura said drily. 'You don't look too bad yourself.'

'Hi girls,' Sarah piped up. We had known Sarah and Ben for what seemed like forever and you rarely saw one without the other. So much so that sometimes people thought they were a couple. They were just the definition of platonic friends. As far as I knew they had never hooked up. Well, not that they had told anyone about anyway.

'Ok, no law-talk tonight,' Ben stated.

'Absolutely!' Sarah exclaimed exuberantly. 'I am *so* over hating what I do and listening to every other lawyer moan. It's just draining. Let's just enjoy tonight and try not to be envious of the fact that Amy has had the guts to give it up.'

After a few more minutes, the taxi pulled up outside the bar.

'This one's on me guys. I think I owe all of you about 5 times over for taxi rides,' said Ben.

'I'm not arguing with that,' I said winking at him before climbing clumsily out of the cab.

The night was spent in a blur of drinking, dancing and having fun. At about 2.30 the Sarah and Ben duo decided that they were going to get a cab home and as I was feeling very tipsy I decided to give the night bus a miss and hop in with them. I reasoned that split between the four of us I'd be able to spring to the taxi fare.

After a short ride home, Laura and I stumbled, giggling towards the front door. As I rooted around for the key, Laura bent and picked something up from the floor.

'Ooh look, a red rose. Looks like one of us has an admirer,' she said drunkenly waving the rose in the air.

'Gotcha!' I said as I pulled the key triumphantly from my bag and after a few attempts managed to get the door open.

'Look at the rose,' Laura demanded, obviously not liking being ignored. She waved it in front of me.

'Who's it for?' I slurred, as I walked unsteadily towards the kitchen. I was longing for some toast.

'Doesn't say,' Laura slurred back as we both kicked off our shoes with sighs of relief. I wiggled my toes to try and get some blood flow back into them.

'Weird,' I said, not really caring who it was for or where it came from. It was probably for Laura since my love life was pretty non-existent. 'Tea and toast?'

'Ooh I would kill for some toast right now. You read my mind.'

In the kitchen, I banged around clumsily, making far more noise than was necessary to make toast and tea. I put the tea pot and buttered toast on a tray and carefully walked towards the sitting room. I noticed that Laura was fast asleep on the sofa, with her mouth open, snoring loudly. She sounded like an airplane taking off. The red rose was strewn on the floor. Very weird I thought. Presumably someone had gotten the house number wrong, I decided. I put a blanket over Laura and settled down, drunkenly staring at Celebrity in the

Jungle, which I never watched when sober, and had a cosy tea and toast for two. Ah I thought in satisfaction. This weekend was making me see life with a bit more perspective. Sometimes I supposed you just needed someone to give you a bit of a shake to see that actually things weren't all that bad. Deciding that I actually didn't care whether the blonde on TV managed to eat donkey's balls, I turned the TV off and went to bed. As I took off my make-up I pondered whether I would ever be able to afford botox and even if I could would I ever actually get it done. I peered into the mirror, examining the skin around my eyes. Must do the lotto, I decided. This was becoming my answer to all my problems. If I won it I imagined that life would be fun and fantastical. Well at the very least I'd be able to afford a coffee without having to budget for it.

Just as I was about to climb into bed, I began to doubt whether I had properly locked the front door. Sighing, I went down the stairs, listening to Laura's snores getting louder and louder as I approached the bottom. I shut both locks properly and only then did I notice a small piece of paper on the door mat, under the small letterbox.

Bending I picked it up and turned it over. It was a small card. The type you get at a florist. On it was scrawled the letter 'K' and written below it were two kiss signs, Xx.

So the rose wasn't for another house. It was obviously for me. It must be from Nick I decided. He was obviously very grateful that I had spent pretty much all of last night at Wandsworth Police Station. What a sweetie, I thought.

I tossed the card in my bin before climbing into bed. I quickly fell into a dreamless sleep.

CHAPTER FIFTEEN

Monday morning saw me once again struggling to ram myself onto the Northern line, while hauling my wheelie bag behind me. A man left on the platform gave me a dirty look, as I managed to get it on just as the doors shut. My bag had taken his place. After doing a quick change in Stockwell to get on the Victoria line, I was thrilled to get a seat. Maybe this week wasn't going to be so bad after all, I thought optimistically.

As I swiped my oyster card at Highbury and Islington station, I saw a familiar frame in front of me. My heart did a little pirouette. Should I just walk casually behind him or hurry to catch up to him? Oh the dilemma. Just stop being an idiot Kate and walk at a normal pace, I chided myself.

After a few paces I was walking beside him. Without wanting to make myself seem creepy, I chirpily said 'Hi Alex!'

He looked around, startled. 'Jesus, Kate, you gave me a fright. I thought it was the homeless guy who was bothering me earlier, back for a second go, having somehow found out my name!'

'I'm glad it's not though,' he added. This was going to keep my brain occupied for a long time. Did he mean that he was glad I wasn't some smelly person asking for money or was he actually happy to see me. Here I went again. I really did read too much into things.

'So do you have much here today?' I questioned.

'A trial for theft of a pedal cycle. Not exactly the crime of the century. I think I might be able to get the Crown to drop it if I get a reasonable prosecutor.'

'Why's that?'

'Well, the police arrive at our house for another unrelated matter and outside the house is this bike which has been reported stolen. So they've charged him with theft. But really there's nothing to link him to stealing this bike, other than the fact that it's found outside his house.'

'Absolutely, anyone could have dumped it there,' I agreed. Both of us knew that it was highly likely that he had stolen the bike, but it was up to the crown to prove, beyond all reasonable doubt that he had and from what Alex was saying they would have difficulty in doing this.

'Did they run forensics on the bike?' I questioned.

'No, which supports my case. I don't think there's enough of a link to go to trial on it. What about you? What are you here for?' he asked as we both hauled our wheelies up the steps, him doing it with far more ease than me.

'I've got two sentencings and a first appearance. I think one of my guys is probably going away today for a while. The court asked for a Pre-Sentence Report to be prepared at the last hearing, despite the fact that from what the client said to me he's perfectly happy to spend some time inside. He wants to get off heroin and feels that the only way he'll be able to do this properly is inside.'

'Poor guy,' Alex said. 'It's always sad at this time of year when clients would rather spend Christmas inside than in the real world. Speaking of Christmas, are you excited about our Christmas party next week? The Chambers have gone all out this year with holly and a Christmas tree and lots of lights!'

'I am,' I said honestly. 'I'm feeling very Christmassy now that we're into December.'

'Well I better go find my client. That is if he has turned up. He has about four Failing to Surrender convictions on his record,' Alex said as he held open the door to the tiny Advocates room. It was already crammed with coats, bags, files and lawyers. The windows were completely fogged up which made it seem even smaller. I unzipped the bag and took out my heels and put my flats in their place. I felt ready for work now. As I sorted through my files, for the morning, I decided that it would be easier to read them in the hallway outside the courtrooms. At least I'd have more room there.

As I settled into a chair, I checked the time. It was 9.40 and none of the courtrooms were open yet. I rolled my eyes. As often happened, it was doubtful that anything would begin at 10.00. Once the usher opened the courtroom door, there could then be a wait for a prosecutor to arrive. There was usually a queue of defence lawyers, behind a harried CPU lawyer, demanding papers, asking if they had reviewed a particular case or any number of other questions that they might have. Usually the Prosecutor had only received their papers an hour or so ago, if even that, and they were expected to be able to answer all our questions. My mother had been really keen for me to work as a Prosecutor. Not because of the morality of what defence lawyers did, but because she saw it as the easier option. In her eyes, Prosecutors, didn't have to do out of hours work, they didn't have to go to police stations late at night. Nor did they have to deal with sometimes very dangerous clients.

What my mum didn't see was what the financial cuts were doing to the Crown Prosecution Service. They had fewer workers to do the same amount of work, which meant that very often files didn't get reviewed or prepared properly for court. I really would hate to be caught up in the Justice system nowadays. The Ministry of Justice had a 'speedy justice' mantra, which very often lead to courts refusing adjournments and other applications, even if it would have been the proper thing to do.

Ten o' clock came and went and still the court room wasn't open. I decided to stroll around and try and find my clients. As I stood, an usher swung open the doors to courtroom one and from the expression on her face I could see that she was loathe to be at work on this Monday morning.

I approached her cautiously, not wanting to irritate her further. I really didn't want to be at court all day and the best way to try and ensure an escape by lunchtime was to play nice with the usher. She wasn't having any of it as I gave her my best smile. She simply ticked off the clients names that I was here to represent and told me grumpily that none of them had checked in with her yet. Which to be fair wasn't really their fault. Even if they were here, she had just made an appearance. I had a quick look inside the courtroom to see whether the Probation officers were in court, so as I could get their reports. No such luck.

I took a walk around the floor, calling out my clients names to see if any of them had turned up. No one yet. I had obviously missed the memo, telling everyone that there was a later start this Monday. Just as I had almost made up my mind to go and get a coffee, a skinny, pale man, with angry looking boils on his chin, approached me.

'You Miss Hunter?' he said in my direction. 'Tommy Wade, your representin' me.'

I plastered a smile on my face. 'Mr. Wade, nice to meet you. Unfortunately the Probation officers aren't in court yet so I don't have your report..' I stopped talking as he interrupted me.

'I didn' go for no appointment. I don't wana be doin' some shit with the Probation officers. I want to go to prison,' he said with emphasis. 'I need to get off the heroin and this is the best thin' for it.'

'Are you sure that's what you want? I can ask the court to consider adjourning the case so as you can have another opportunity to meet with the Probation officers?'

'Nah-it's not goin' to work. Only thin' that works for me is to go off it in jail. Done it before all by meself,' he said somewhat proudly.

I didn't tell him that he obviously could do with some outside help as he was back on it again.

'If that's what you want Mr. Wade. Check yourself in with the usher and with a bit of luck we'll be called on soon.'

As he walked away, I looked in pity at his emaciated frame. My guess was that he would probably succeed in not using heroin while in prison. However on release, having no support network at all he would probably end up back on the drug. Prison really was a revolving door for so many.

As I tried to find my other two clients, a lady wearing what looked suspiciously like pyjamas and imitation Uggs walked in a straight line towards me.

'I need to get on as soon as possible right, I'm needin' to get back to my childr'n at home.'

'Sorry, and you are?' I questioned.

'Tracey Dixon. You from HBW?' she asked sounding exasperated.

'Yes, I'm Miss Hunter. You're here for sentencing but the Probation officers aren't in court yet so we'll have to wait for them to arrive before I can discuss your report with you.'

As expected she didn't take this well. 'Why the fuck do I have to wait on 'em? I fucking turned up 't court on time. I got things to do ain't I?'

I opted not to tell her that actually she hadn't arrived at court until after 10.30 and if court had started on time a warrant could have been issued for her arrest.

Instead I said, 'I know it's frustrating Tracy but hopefully they'll arrive soon. In fact I'll go check again right now.'

'Alright so.' She seemed slightly placated. 'I'm goin' out for a fag,' she looked at me defiantly almost daring me to tell her not to.

'Ok but don't go far. Don't want you to have to wait around all day now. Being so busy and all,' I couldn't help adding.

She scowled at me and turned her back waddling off in the direction of the exit. Honestly I thought, how did some people have so little respect for the legal system that they turned up to court in their pyjamas and a hoody.

My third client seemed to be a no-show at the moment, so I went in search of the Probation officer again so as I could get Tracy's report. This time I was in luck. Court had started so I bowed at the Magistrates as I entered the courtroom and walked quietly around the back of the room towards the Probation officer.

'Tracy Dixon,' I whispered. 'Can I have her report? I'm also representing Mr. Wade. He'll be a non-report as he didn't turn up for his appointment with you. He wants to go to prison to get clean.'

The probation officer rolled her eyes and smiled at me. She had heard it all before. She handed me Tracy's report and I mouthed thanks. I walked back the way I had come, reading through the report as I went. I flicked straight to the back which was the part which gave the sentencing recommendation to the court.

They were recommending 120 hours unpaid work for her. Oh she was going to love that! How would she manage to get herself dressed and to her placement on time? My guess is that she wouldn't and that there was a good chance that I'd be seeing her back here after Christmas for breach of her Community order.

Later that day as I put on my flats and chucked my files into my bag I wondered if Alex was still around. I was lucky that I was getting out of here just before lunchtime. On the down side it meant that I would be back in the office for my afternoon appointment. I hadn't met the client before but I knew the rough background to his case, as Nick had represented him at the police station. He had been so repulsed by the client that he refused to deal with him now and unfortunately Basil had given the file to me. It was a historic sex abuse allegation and to say that I wasn't looking forward to the consultation was an understatement.

Just in case I did bump into Alex as I was leaving, I checked myself in my compact and applied some lipgloss. Hauling the wheelie down the stairs I began thinking of what I wanted for lunch. My stomach was rumbling and the ham salad sandwiches I had made this morning were probably limp and soggy by now. As I was close to the first floor I could feel my phone vibrating in my coat pocket. I fumbled to get it out and as I did, my grip slipped on the wheelie and it thudded to the bottom. Oh well, that saved me some backache! It was an unknown number. For a moment, I let myself believe that it was Alex phoning to see if I wanted to get some lunch together. I deliberated whether or not to answer the call, as my conversation with Nick flashed through my head. I decided to go for it.

'Hello, Miss Hunter speaking.'

The reply was an angry tirade. 'Why the fuck was Scott charged. How the fuck did I not find out until this morning eh? What type of fucking lawyer are you eh?'

Although I had an idea who was on the other line, I asked anyway.

'It's Scott fucking Ryan's father,' as though it was the most obvious thing in the world.

I took a deep breath, as I bent down to pick up my

wheelie bag.

'Mr. Ryan, the reason you weren't contacted about the fact that Scott was charged with GBH was because you didn't give me your phone number.' I knew this would incense Mr. Ryan. Why was he suddenly so interested in his son's welfare anyway? He hadn't even spared a few hours of his precious time to be present at his son's taped interview.

'That's fucking ridiculous,' he yelled. I held the phone away from my ear and I could still hear him breathing heavily. He was obviously furious and from the way he had slurred some words I was guessing that he had already been drinking. Something suddenly occurred to me.

'Mr. Ryan,' I said as politely as I could manage after being cursed at for the last few minutes. 'How did you get my number?'

'Your fucking office gave it to me. Some fucking use you are though. A waste of my bloody phone credit.'

Before I could tell him that it was extremely important that he attended court with Scott the line went dead.

No matter how many times I asked the receptionists not to give out my personal phone number, my requests seemed to fall on deaf ears. I gritted my teeth and gave my wheelie a kick to vent some frustration.

'Whoa, bad morning in court Kate?' came a voice from behind me on the stairs.

Damn, I thought. I must look nuts kicking my file bag. I turned towards Alex. I wasn't the calm, collected, glossy lipped person I had hoped I would be, if I bumped into him. Instead my cheeks were red from anger and he had just seen me acting like a petulant child.

'Just venting some frustration,' I said truthfully.

'Yes, far safer than kicking a client,' he said, with a wink.

'How about I buy you a sandwich and you can tell me all about it?' Was it my imagination or did he look hopeful.

'That would be lovely,' I smiled. The ham sandwiches were probably a ball of warm bread, ham and tinfoil I reasoned, especially after my wheelies trip down the stairs.

CHAPTER SIXTEEN

'He did what?' I squealed, almost spitting some of my brie, walnut and grape ciabatta over Alex.

'I know! All he had to say was that he didn't take the bike. Instead he decided to come clean on the stand. Well, actually, I think he was too dumb to know what he was doing!'

'I was going to say I can't believe it, but actually I can. Do you think he realises that he convicted himself?'

'Not at all and it's not as though it was his first ever trial. It's probably about his fourth. Obviously the prosecutor was thrilled as he did her job for her!'

'So what did he get?' I asked before popping the rest of the ciabatta into my mouth. 'Mmmh,' I said in satisfaction before I could help myself.

'Enjoy that?' Alex asked looking amused.

'Absolutely delicious.'

'It's adjourned for a Pre-Sentence report. I imagine he'll get unpaid work. He's in breach of a conditional discharge as well because of this conviction, but they might leave that run as it's almost near its end.' A conditional discharge was sometimes given for a fixed period of time, as a form of sentence. It effectively meant that a client would not be sentenced that day in court but if they were convicted of another offence while the conditional discharge was still in place they could then be sentenced for the original offence.

'The Prosecutor must be thrilled that she didn't agree to drop it,' I remarked.

'That's the funny thing. I think that she was ready to bin it but the Officer in the case refused to give his okay to it,' he said wiping his lips with his napkin.

'So what are you up to for the afternoon?' I

117

questioned, changing the subject to a non-work related one.

'Work, I'm afraid,' he said looking dejected. 'I have a four day three handed youth robbery trial starting tomorrow. It almost seems that my life revolves around youth robbery trials at the moment.'

Well that hadn't been a very successful attempt at changing the subject.

'What about you?' he asked. 'Are you back in the office?'

'Unfortunately. I have a consultation with a client about historic sexual assault charges,' I grimaced.

'No doubt he'll be pleading not guilty,' Alex said. 'It's so rare for someone to plead guilty to being a sex offender.'

'You're right. Nick represented him at the station and from what he says it sounds like there is a lot of evidence against him. Nick said he's belligerent, stubborn and not willing to take advice at all. I can't wait,' I groaned.

'Well don't let me hold you!' Alex grinned, checking his watch. 'I suppose I better get back to chambers and hopefully the solicitors will have forwarded my brief for tomorrow.'

We both stood, gathering our things and I followed after him, weaving through the tables and manoeuvring the wheelie behind me.

'Right,..well...erm, I guess I'll see you next week at your Christmas party,' I smiled, racking my brain for something else to say.

'Absolutely, bring your mistletoe.' He smiled at me causing my heart to go crazy.

'Go easy on your bag,' he said over his shoulder, as he strolled down the street. I almost hugged myself there and then. I was falling badly and life seemed wonderful all of a sudden. The Christmas lights seemed brighter, the carols less annoying and the air seemed crisper. Also I was being a lot more pleasant to people I realised, as I side stepped to allow a mum struggling with a pram and a young child to get past. I felt like doing something Christmassy. Instead I resigned myself to the fact that I would be spending the afternoon, trapped in my office with a nightmare client. My mood only slightly dulled I made my way towards the tube, for once not minding having to haul my wheelie behind me.

That afternoon at four o' clock the dreaded client still hadn't turned up. I was sitting drinking tea, while trying not to surf the net (ie stalk Alex on facebook) and do some paperwork. He was a half an hour late and I was getting hopeful that he may not turn up.

At quarter past four, I was feeling quite jubilant about the fact that it was almost certain that he was going to be a no-show. I was just about to go and get another cup of tea, when there was a knock on the door. My heart sank.

'Come in,' I called.

A stooped man, with a craggy face poked his head around the door.

'Nick Cannon 'ere?' he asked with a croaky West Country accent.

'Are you Mr. Phillips?'

'I might be,' he said cagily.

God it frustrated me when they insisted on being cryptic. He was at his own solicitor's office. Did he think I had a wire linked up directly to Scotland Yard. Calm Kate, calm. I took a deep breath. I was getting very good at taking a deep breath before losing my rag at a client.

'Well if you are, your appointment is with me. My name is Miss Hunter,' I said briskly. 'You can take a seat here,' I said gesturing to the empty chair in front of my desk.

'I'm 'ere to see Mr. Cannon,' he said stubbornly. I decided not to tell him that he *would* be seeing Nick if he hadn't been such a royal pain in the ass at the police station.

'I'm afraid Nick has been held up at court,' I lied. 'Nick has asked me to have a consultation with you. I assure you, I'm fully aware of your situation,' I said sitting opposite him and placing my hand on his file which lay on my desk.

I looked into his watery eyes. The part which should have been white was an off yellow colour.

'I don't want to be dealin' with a woman solicitor,' he said not bothering to hide his disgust. I had experienced this before, particularly in sex cases. All I could do was try and reassure him that I was on his side and that he could feel confident that I wasn't going to judge him.

'Also Mr. Phillips, obviously anything you tell me is confidential and protected by Lawyer/client privilege. I do urge you to be as truthful as you can with me as this will allow me to advise you properly.'

I hoped I had convinced him. I really didn't want to have to tell Basil that the client had walked. I hadn't seen him since falling *at* him the other day and I wasn't really in any rush to either.

'Are you happy for me to continue Mr. Phillips?'

''suppose so,' he said somewhat petulantly.

I decided to state the obvious at the outset. 'Well you will be aware that you've been charged with 6 counts of sexual assault and 2 counts of rape?'

'Load of bloody lies,' was his response.

I had never had a client admit to charges of this sort, unless they pleaded on the day of the trial, in order to get a slightly reduced sentence. Everyone hates sex offenders and no-one wants to admit to being one.

Well it seemed like he wasn't going to bolt out the door in the immediate future so I decided to go for gold and start talking about the charges.

'I know, from speaking to Nick *at length,* about your case, that this is the first time that you have been charged with an offence.' My 'at length' discussion had taken place in the kitchen while we bickered over who would get the last tea bag, but Mr. Phillips didn't need to know that.

'Too right it is,' his Devon accent appeared stronger, as he seemed to relax around me.

'Well let me explain how this will work. You have been bailed to attend Westminster Magistrates Court on the 18th January at 9.30am.' I leafed through the pile of papers in front of me, looking through Nick's notes from the police station.

'Your bail, has conditions attached. These are not to contact the girls mentioned in the charges either directly or indirectly. This was probably explained to you at the police station but just to emphasise the point, this means that you can't contact them by text, facebook or use any other method to contact them.'

'I got no reason to contact any of 'em,' he almost growled.

I sat back in my chair and looked him squarely in the eyes. I really wasn't in the mood for a belligerent client. He stared back at me and seemed to thaw just a little.

'What's goin' to 'appen in court on the 18th?' he asked eventually. He sounded a lot more civil now. Progress, I thought.

'Well, Mr. Phillips.'

'Call me Bob.'

'Ok, Bob, these charges are matters which are deemed too serious to proceed in the Magistrates Court.

However all matters have the first hearing listed in the Magistrates Court. On the 18th, you will appear before the court. You will be asked to give your name and address by the Court Clerk. Then, because of the serious nature of these charges they will be sent to the Crown Court.'

'What 'appens at the Crown Court then?'

'Well the first date at the Crown Court will be called a Plea and Case Management Hearing. This is basically when the Court will take your plea's to the charges and the court will make directions about when the Prosecution must serve certain information on us. A trial will then take place at a later date, possibly about 8 weeks after that listing.'

'So I gotta worry 'bout all this 'til well into next year do I?'

'I'm afraid there's a definite procedure attached to legal affairs, Bob and there's no avenue to speed it up in this case.'

'Alright then.' He sat back looking defeated.

'On the 18th the Crown will serve Advanced Information on us. Essentially this is the evidence they have against you. Until that point, and until we know exactly what the allegations are against you it's very difficult to discuss the matter in depth with you.'

'Is that all you can tell me so today?' he said, looking as though he was getting irritated again.

'I'm afraid so Bob.'

'Why did I need to come into the office so? I had to get two buses and a train to get 'ere. Why was I put to all that trouble eh?'

'Well Bob it's my understanding that you requested an appointment to see a lawyer,' I answered calmly.

'Well I wouldn't have done if I'd 'ave known that, that is all you were going to tell me. I coulda found that out on google without 'avin to take any busses or train.'

I held back a sigh. There was a note on his file, from the receptionist who had made the appointment, stating that she had explained that a lawyer wouldn't be able to do much without the Advanced information but that the client had requested this appointment anyway.

I didn't want to get into an argument. Also I really didn't need to piss off Basil by losing the client.

'Well Bob,' I said with false brightness, 'at least we've met and you now have a very clear idea of what's going to take place on the 18th. What we could do today if you like is to go through in detail each charge against you and what you would like to say in response to the charges.'

'Nah,' he said. 'Let's wait until we get those papers. What did you call them?'

'The advanced information,' I replied.

I took one of my business cards from my top drawer and handed it to him. 'Please don't hesitate to call me if you have any other questions.'

I stood, hoping that this would encourage him to do the same. I was in luck. He took hold of his walking stick which lay resting against the desk and stood, putting all his weight on the stick. He hobbled towards the door. He turned before he left the room.

'I didn't do it you know. I didn't do anything wrong.'

I stayed silent. What could I say to that?

He turned slowly and huffed out of the room. I sat back on my chair. Was he the one? Was he the first innocent man I was going to represent? I had been acquitted at trials, but that didn't necessarily mean that the clients had been innocent. It generally meant that the Crown couldn't prove the case beyond all reasonable doubt.

Moments later, Nick appeared with a wide grin on his face. 'How'd it go?'

'You owe me more than the last tea-bag,' I replied.

'How about a Starbucks then?' he asked, hitting my weak spot. 'How about one of those hot special Christmas drinks you like?'

'Well if you threw in a chocolate cookie or brownie you'd earn bonus points.'

'It's a deal. Grab your coat. Don't say I don't know how to treat a lady.'

Just then my phone rang. Nick held the door for me as I answered. 'Hey Laura. You must be buzzing with excitement. Are you getting any work done or are you just googling Bali?'

Laura was off on her 'fix her life' trip tomorrow.

'I'm not doing a thing!' she whispered.

'Listen Kate, I was just ringing to see if you wanted to do a cheap and cheerful dinner tonight. On me,' she added.

'Are you sure?' I asked.

'Absolutely, I want to get my holiday off to a great start. Plus I won't see you for ten whole days. How about Strada on Southbank at 7.30?'

'Perfect.'

'See you there,' she whispered and hung up.

Nick and I were already outside Starbucks. 'Why don't you grab a table and I'll get us our drinks. Which sugary sweet liquid would you like?' He asked with a grin.

'A praline latte and shortbread cookie would be perfect, thanks.'

I found us a cosy table in the corner and when Nick was settled and I had thanked him for the coffee, we fell into a comfortable silence as we nibbled on our cookies and sipped our coffees.

After a couple of moments, Nick broke the silence, 'So what do you think of the new out of hours pay?'

'Emily mentioned something about that the other day, but I haven't heard anything formal about it. What have you heard about it?' I asked. I could feel a mild panic building in my stomach.

'Well, did you get Basil's email this afternoon?' Nick questioned.

I hadn't checked my emails since before meeting with Mr. Phillips earlier.

'I take it from your face that you haven't checked your mail. Sorry to be the bearer of bad news.'

'S'ok,' I mumbled through a mouthful of cookie. 'I was going to find out sometime.'

'You know Kate, that you're welcome to any of my out of hours work, to make up your pay, if that would make things any easier for you?'

Tears pricked my eyes. Stop being such a baby Kate, I chastised myself.

'Nick you really are a gem, thank you. I suppose what's bothering me is that I already feel shattered from the amount of out of hours I'm doing and to have to do more on top of that would mean that effectively, law would become my entire life.'

'I know,' Nick said his eyes full of sympathy. He knew that he was in a very lucky position, not having to worry about pay cuts. He was one of the few lawyers who seemed to find enjoyment in their jobs-but that could be because he only did the bare 9-5.

I suppose what I'm really irritated about is that we just signed over our duty slots to them for the next six months and then they introduced the new changes. They *had* to have known that they were going to do this when we were signing them over. What do you think?'

'Of course they did. They did what all law firms seem to be doing at the moment and royally screwed us over. I know I'm in a very lucky position, in that I don't need to rely on out of hours work but for everyone else, it's a really tough cut.'

'Well, there's no use sitting here moaning about it,' I said draining my cup. 'As usual I have a mountain of paperwork to get through.'

Nick sighed. 'Back to it then, I suppose.' As we buttoned our coats and walked out into the cold something occurred to me.

'By the way Nick, there was no need to leave me a rose for doing your out of hours work. I much rather thank you's which take the form of food.'

He turned towards me. 'What *are* you talking about Kate Hunter? Have you lost the plot? I didn't give you a rose.'

'Ya right,' I said looking at him intently, to try and work out if he was joking or not.

'Honestly, Kate, I didn't send you a rose. Was there a card attached to it?'

'Yes, it just said K, XX. Are you serious that you didn't put a rose on our doorstep?'

'Kate, I'm smooth, but I'm not that smooth.'

'Who the hell left the rose on the doorstep then?' I mused out loud.

'Ooh Kate has a secret admirer,' Nick sing-songed as we walked up the steps to the office.

Hmm, I wondered to myself. Could my love life be picking up after all?

When we entered our office, Nick sat at his desk and began doing the times crossword. I started daydreaming about what knight in shining armour could have left the rose on my doorstep. Logically it had to be someone who knew where I lived, or at the very least had made efforts to find out where I lived. An image of Alex floated into my mind. In my fantasy, I saw him sneaking up our drive and stealthily placing the rose on the doorstep, before hastily making off.

Nick broke my reverie. 'Kate, what is the egg-white

called again,' he asked.

'The albumen'

'Oh ya, albumen,' Nick said slowly as he wrote it into the crossword grid.

'Fantasising about your secret admirer were you? I know you too well Kate. Can't get anything past me'

' Of course I wasn't. I was thinking of how to respond to the CPS on this file.'

'So what file is that then?' Nick asked evilly.

'Em,' I said trying to buy myself some time, as my eyes flitted over the papers on my desk.

'Barron,' I blurted out. 'John Barron's file,' I said feeling rather pleased with myself.

'Didn't that conclude last week when I attended for sentence?'

Crap. 'Okay. Okay,' I relented. 'I was daydreaming about the rose. Happy?' I grumbled.

'Extremely happy. Once again, super psychic Nick has been proved right,' he said tapping his temples with his forefingers.

I glanced at the clock at the bottom of my computer. 6.30. I suppose I *could* do some work for the next half hour before I had to leave to meet Laura. I reluctantly looked at the pile on the left hand side of my desk. It suddenly occurred to me that I should start at the bottom of the pile as those letters had been there the longest. I almost felt like patting myself on the back. It felt like such a genius idea. How had I not thought of this before?

Cautiously I pulled out a letter from the bottom of the pile, willing it not to topple.

'What are you doing Kate?' Nick asked curiously from across the room, evidently bored with the crossword. 'Playing correspondence jenga?'

'It just occurred to me that the letters at the bottom of this pile have been there the longest so I should probably look at them first.'

'Hmm. You never cease to surprise me! That's actually a good idea.' He eyed his pile of post. 'I think I'll tackle it tomorrow though. I promised Milly I would go Christmas shopping with her this evening. Even that's more appealing that getting stuck into *that*,' he said with a grimace, gesturing towards a mass of paper, which looked dangerously close to toppling off his desk, if someone sneezed too hard.

After Nick had left, I settled down in peace and began to make inroads into the post. Oh for the days when firms could afford secretaries I sighed. Now I had to do everything from typing my own letters, filing, meeting with clients *and* go to court and the police stations. My dictaphone, lay covered in dust, in the bottom drawer of my desk. Maybe I could ebay it I mused, as I reached for the next letter.

It was a handwritten and I immediately recognised the scrawled writing. I smiled to myself. Poor Shane, I thought. He must be really lonely, if he keeps writing to me. This letter was on the same paper as before and was equally as brief.

Kate,

I realy want to see you again. You were a big help to me. I need someone on my side. No one seems to care about me.

Shane.

Xx

Apart from one spelling mistake, his writing was definitely coming on. There was the addition of two kisses at the bottom which hadn't been there before. He must be lonely around Christmas time I thought to myself, before balling up the letter and tossing it into the bin.

Realising that I had spent longer than I had intended absorbed in the paperwork, I stood, not bothering to turn off my computer and hurriedly pulled on my coat as I walked out the door.

By the time I made it to Southbank I was 15 minutes late and flushed from rushing. Laura was seated already and sipping a glass of red wine from the bottle which was on the table. As I approached, she stood and flung her arms around me exuberantly.

As we were sitting, a waiter arrived with bread and olives. 'Oh I ordered us some nibbles. I'm *starving!*'

'Probably because you've hardly been eating, since you booked your holiday,' I said wryly.

'I know, I know,' she conceded, 'but it seems so long since I was in a bikini that I felt I needed to take measures. It really is such a pity fudging Basil wouldn't allow you to take the time off,' she said her excitement waning temporarily.

'I can't even think about going,' I said. 'It makes me too angry,' I added as I tore off a piece of bread and dipped it in some olive oil.

'How was work?' Laura questioned in an attempt to change the subject. 'Probably not the best choice of subject is it?' she said realising her mistake.

As the conversation became more light-hearted and I began to sip the wine I could feel my shoulders relax and some of the day's tension slip away. By the time the bill arrived, I was only feeling the tiniest bit jealous of Laura's holiday.

'Ok, we're getting a cab tonight,' Laura stated, as we walked into the cold night air. She said it in that way of hers which meant that there was no arguing with her.

'I feel like I've started my holiday and I don't want to walk in the freezing cold to the tube,' she said as she stuck out her hand to hail a cab. As we clambered in, my phone buzzed in my coat pocket.

It was a text from Emily.

Can u attend Vauxhall Police Station for interview? Ready now?

I sighed. Emily loved highlighting the fact that I was so much poorer than her and needed to attend the Police stations at the most annoying and inconvenient times, just to make ends meet.

No can do, I typed. *Just had wine.*

I considered writing something else, but decided to leave it at that. There was no point in pretending that we were actually friends.

I hadn't been expecting a reply but one came back almost as soon as I had pressed the send button.

Ooh and I thought you were on the breadline!Enjoy!

Sarcastic bitch, I thought angrily.

'What's wrong?' Laura asked, 'Basil?'

'No, not this time. Just Emily being a bitch.'

'So she's still the same then.' Laura had gone to boarding school with Emily and from what I had heard it sounded that if anything Emily had become more venomous with age.

'Let's not spoil our evening by talking about her,' I said and asked Laura a question about the spa in her hotel to change the subject. She chatted animatedly as we drove towards Clapham. I tried to hand Laura some money for the taxi as we pulled up outside our house. She waved my hand away while handing some notes to the driver. I pushed open the car door, almost taking out a cyclist in the process. I let Laura climb out first and the cyclist unleashed a tirade of abuse at her.

Red-faced Laura turned to face me. 'Thanks for

that,' she said sarcastically, but from the glint in her eye I could tell that she didn't really mind. She was too excited about her trip.

'So what time is your flight?' I asked as we walked to the front door.

'Early o' clock. I'll have to be up at five. Hey, what's this?' she exclaimed as I rummaged in my bag for the door keys.

As I put the key in the door and did the customary throw my body weight at it, I saw out of the corner of my eye that Laura was holding a single red rose. Once again I fell into the hallway as the door flew open.

'Is there a card?' I questioned as I shut the door behind us.

'Yep. It says, hey it's for you!'

'Let me see,' I said as I grabbed the card from her hand.

'Ooh Kate has a secret admirer,' Laura said laughing as she headed into the kitchen for some water. I could hear the tap running as I read the card. It was very similar to the last one. It was plain white with a little flower in the top left hand corner. The words ' *Kate, u mean d world 2 me Xx'*, were written on the remaining space.

There was something about it that sent shivers down my spine. I couldn't imagine an admirer who was sending a genuine rose and flower would use text speak. The writing seemed oddly familiar as well but I couldn't place it.

'Who do you think it's from?' Laura said emerging from the kitchen.

'No idea. But I imagine it's a joke of some sort. Look at the way the words are written. Hardly the scrawl of someone trying to make an impression!'

'Well it's definitely not Shakespeare I'll give you that. Anyway I need to go pack and get some sleep.'

'Oh Laura have an absolutely fantastic time,' I said as I engulfed her in a hug. 'It'll be strange here without you.'

Laura turned before she reached the top of the stairs.

'Kate, at Alex's Christmas party, don't act like you usually do around guys you really like. Act like yourself!'

With that, she disappeared into her room, leaving me standing open mouthed at the foot of the stairs. Fleetingly I wondered if he was the admirer sending me the roses. As much as I wanted it to be him, I quickly dismissed the idea as ludicrous. I would have hoped that Alex could produce something a little more eloquent than what was scrawled on my card. Deciding that it was all probably a joke of some sort which would reveal itself in time, I tossed the card in the bin and got ready for bed.

As I curled up, I thought about what Laura's last words to me had been. She was right. I usually did act like an idiot version of myself around guys I really liked. I was *so* looking forward to his chambers party at the end of this week. I fell asleep imagining what hairstyle would go with the dress.

CHAPTER SEVENTEEN

The next morning, I arrived on time at Charing Cross police station, to attend the re-interview of Ted Galvin. Once again, he was sitting in the corner of the reception area, looking pale and completely out of place. He was nervously eyeing up a couple of black youths who seemed on the verge of getting into a fight. Their voices were getting louder and louder. Ted pressed himself against the wall and closed his eyes. He looked like he was trying to transport himself out of the station. Not going to happen Ted, I thought to myself as I approached him. He looked thinner than before and had deep circles under his eyes.

He leapt to his feet when he saw me and stretched out his hand.

'Mr. Galvin, how are you doing?' I asked while shaking his clammy hand.

'Please Kate, call me Ted. I'm not very well to be honest. I haven't slept properly since the last time I was here. It's all I can think about. I can't work. I can't eat and my wife, God bless her, definitely knows something is up. What's going to happen today Kate?' he asked anxiously.

His eyes were pools of worry and fear of the unknown.

'Ted, I spoke with Officer Leadberry yesterday evening to try and ascertain what he wants to question you about today.'

Ted was hanging on my every word.

'It turns out that Rebecca *is* in fact pregnant, which accords with your story. The officer wants to ask you some more questions about this. What I need to warn you about though is that they may be thinking of bailing you for quite a while. They may feel that a decision cannot be made until the baby is born and proper DNA testing can be done.'

'So they still think I raped her?'

I got the feeling that Ted had been clinging to the hope that this would all be dropped today. I didn't have a chance to answer his question because Officer Leadberry appeared.

'Hello Miss Hunter. Mr. Galvin,' he said nodding at each of us in turn. 'Thank you for both arriving promptly. There has been a very interesting development this morning with regards to this file. If you would both like to follow me through to a consultation room and I can explain it all more fully to you.'

He held the door open for both of us and we walked through. Teds breathing was laboured and I could see a sheen of sweat on his forehead. I wondered what this new development was. Yesterday evening the Officer had been adamant that it would be a standard re-interview.

We settled ourselves in a consultation room and Officer Leadberry sat before us, opening a large file. 'This won't take long, I assure you.' I nodded at him urging him to continue.

'Well,' he continued. 'It turns out that you were telling the truth Mr. Galvin.' He sat back in his chair with his hands clasped on the table in front of him.

'Rebecca attended the police station early this morning and retracted her previous statement of complaint to the police. Apparently when her parents didn't react as badly as she had thought they would to her being pregnant, she decided that she should come clean.'

I looked side-ways at Ted. Tears were streaming down his face. Of relief I presumed. His life had been turned upside down for the last number of weeks. I couldn't imagine the burden which had just been lifted from his shoulders. He had suffered through endless sleepless nights and weeks of worry.

'We are terribly sorry for any inconvenience this may have caused you Mr. Galvin, but as a police force we have to investigate to the best of our ability any complaint made to us.'

Ted snorted. 'You have no idea,' was all he said. He took a deep breath, seemed to compose himself and stood. 'If that's all, I'll be leaving then?'

'Yes, yes of course,' the Officer said hurriedly.

I stood and accompanied Mr. Galvin to the front reception area.

'Kate, I have no idea how to thank you,' he said gratitude dripping from his words.

I simply smiled at him. 'Ted, you've got your life back. If we ever meet again, hopefully it'll be in better circumstances.'

'I just have one question Kate. Will this appear on any records the police hold?'

'Well you certainly won't have any criminal record or anything of that sort Ted. The police records will show that you were interviewed about the rape allegation. However it will also show the outcome of the investigation and the fact that the complainant withdrew her statement.'

He nodded happily at me. A broad smile lit up his face and he turned and walked out the door. His shoulders already looked less hunched. What a strange turn of events I thought.

I decided to walk back to the office as it was such a bright crisp day. I thought of Ted as I strolled and wondered if the police would take any action against the complainant for making false allegations. Probably not I decided, especially because of her age and as she was pregnant. What an ordeal for Ted to have to go through I mused.

As I was almost at the tube, my phone buzzed. I glanced at the screen before answering it.

'Siswa! How was the Big Apple? Was it amazing?'

'Sis, hey! Oh Kate I can't tell you how much fun it was. I loved every minute of it,' she said excitedly. 'How have you been doing? Anything exciting?'

'Oh you know, same 'ol same 'ol. Nothing new to report here. I can't wait to see you at Christmas for a proper catch-up.'

'Oh I know, me too,' she replied. 'It's crazy that we both live in London but see so little of eachother.

'I know. We'll have to make a new years resolution to see more of eachother next year! Did you have any luck with Dad's birthday present by the way?'

'Well sis, I was thinking loads about it. What do you think about getting himself and Mum a weekend away somewhere? You know, so they can create some memories. He pretty much has everything that he wants. I was thinking that £500 each from you, me and James should cover it? What d'you think?' she asked anxiously. 'I can cover your share, if you like,' she added hurriedly.

'I think that's a fabulous idea sis. Don't be silly. Thanks for the offer but I can cover the £500. No worries at all.' My mind went into overdrive calculating how many out of hours police station attendances I would have to cover to make up the £500.

'Sis I'm just about to hop on the tube. I'll chat to you later. Love you!'

As I sat in the tube, I came to the conclusion that I would have to swallow my pride and ask Emily if I could cover any police station attendances that she didn't want to do. After all, desperate times call for desperate measures.

The rest of the week passed in a blur of court attendances and far too many interviews at various police stations at ungodly hours. I seemed to have spent my nights, hopping blindly out of bed, pulling on clothes and hoping that I might grab a bit more sleep before I had to be at court. My days were spent surviving on copious amounts of coffee and trying to be as functional as possible on barely any sleep. I watched the circles under my eyes deepen as I approached Friday. The plus side was that I was some way towards making up the £500 for my Dads present. On the down side I awoke on Friday morning, to the annoying continuous beeping of my phone alarm, feeling shattered. I had only had two hours sleep and I had a horrendous headache. My eyes were glued together and my tongue was stuck to the roof of my mouth. Why did I feel as though I had a God awful hangover? The week of no sleep had caught up on me and I had one hour to sort myself out and get to City of London Magistrates Court.

I stared at myself in the bathroom mirror wondering how I was going to make myself look presentable for Alex's chambers Christmas party tonight. My eyes were bloodshot, my hair limp and there didn't seem to be any colour in my face. Hoping that a shower and a few espressos would sort me out, I willed my body to function at normal speed. Today's harassment trial was going to be difficult to get through.

CHAPTER EIGHTEEN

That evening as I tried to coax my hair into what I hoped were sexy curls, I stifled yawns in between drinking from my gin and tonic, which was more gin than tonic. I had to admit that I had done an extremely good job with my makeup application and I certainly looked more alive than when I had started the process. Laura's dress fitted perfectly and the silver flecks on the black fabric really caught the light. The low back made me feel sexy and with a bit of luck Alex would think so too. The more gin I was consuming, the better I was feeling about the night. I felt an excited flutter in my stomach. My mobile buzzed with a text from Sarah,

In taxi. Should be at yours in about 10.x

Excellent, time for one more G&T I thought.

As I put the finishing touches to my make-up I danced around singing to the music coming from my I-pod. The gin was definitely getting me in a party mood.

When I heard the taxi beep, I drained my glass, grabbed my clutch and headed out into the cold.

As I climbed into the taxi, Sarah and Ben were animatedly discussing who would end up shagging who tonight. Ferndale Chambers were notorious for their Christmas parties and even though most other firms and chambers were making severe cutbacks, they continued as though it was the good 'ol days. I could only imagine what our office was thinking of doing for the Christmas party. If they could find a place which did a 'Bring your own Bottle night', I'm sure we would be having it there.

'So what do you think?' Sarah asked me. 'Do you think this is the year Basil will get lucky?'

'Ugh, gross Sarah! I don't think *anyone* could *ever* be drunk enough to go there.' The thought repulsed me.

The taxi pulled up outside the chambers and as I handed Sarah money for the cab, I felt a flutter in my stomach.

Inside, people who I normally saw in dull suits were dressed elegantly and were milling about laughing and chatting, holding champagne flutes and wine glasses. Alex had been right about the Christmas decorations. The Chambers certainly had gone all out this year. A Christmas tree touched the high ceiling in the foyer and was covered in twinkling lights. The banister of the sweeping staircase had wreaths of holly and red bows wrapped around it. There was a string quartet playing in the corner. How could they afford all this when a lot of firms weren't even having the most meagre of Christmas parties I wondered?

As we made our way towards the bar, I could see Basil propped up against the counter talking at some person who had the misfortune to want a drink at the same time as him. Not wanting to be anywhere near frazzled Basil tonight I asked Sarah to get me a drink. I surreptitiously looked around wondering if Alex was here yet.

As the hours ticked by, people got more and more drunk and the elegance of earlier gave way to more raucous behaviour. People became less stealthy about the fact that they were heading off to shag someone other than their husband or wife. I began to wonder if Alex was here at all. As I was contemplating leaving I saw him walk into the room in his black overcoat. The butterflies in my stomach went berserk. The combination of this, all the booze and extreme tiredness suddenly hit me. Crap. My stomach was churning. I was going to be sick. I turned and fled to the nearest toilet. I completely skipped the queue and launched myself into a vacant cubicle, just in time. I spent the next ten minutes throwing up.

When I finally felt well enough to emerge from the cubicle and return to the party I was glad that everyone else was completely blitzed. No-one had taken any notice of my sprint to the ladies. With the exception of Alex, who I was sure had seen me before I took off.

I went in search of my coat, deciding that it was time to call it a night. As I was handing my ticket into the cloakroom, hoping to make a speedy exit, I heard an all too familiar voice behind me. I inwardly cringed. I knew without having to turn around that it was Alex.

I felt his hand on my shoulder. 'Kate, are you okay? Someone said you were feeling ill?'

As my coat was handed to me, I turned around to look him in the eyes. 'Turns out a week of no sleep and huge quantities of alcohol aren't a good mixture after all!' I joked, hoping to make light of the situation.

'Well I'm glad you're okay,' he said sounding genuinely concerned and not at all like he was going to take the piss out of me, which I was grateful for. 'I would ask if you would like to get a drink but that's probably not the best idea. How about a coffee? I know a room with a coffee machine which is closed off for the party?'

'Sure,' I said softly, 'that would be lovely.'

As Alex tinkered about with the coffee machine, I stole a glance at my face in my compact. Thankfully not too much damage had been caused by my 10 minutes in the bathroom. I stuffed it back quickly into my clutch as Alex looked as though he was finished with barista duties. He turned around with two mugs of steaming coffee.

'I remembered from our lunch that you like it strong

so I put in an extra shot to yours,' he said handing me a mug.

'That's perfect,' I said contentedly as I took a sip.

We sat in easy silence for a few moments and any humiliation I had felt earlier was gone. I could hear the noise from the party outside the door and I felt as though we were in our own little cocoon in here. The room looked like it was the chambers library. It was all dark wood, dim reading lights, and the walls were lined from floor to ceiling with shelves of books. The whole effect was very cosy.

'I was hoping to get to spend some time with you tonight,' Alex said suddenly in a soft voice. So soft, I doubted whether I had heard him correctly. Laura's voice floated into my head. Don't act like an idiot at Alex's Christmas party, had been her sage words before she had left for Bali.

'Me too,' I said just as quietly. 'I thought you hadn't come tonight,' I added.

'I almost didn't make it.' He didn't add why. Without warning he took the coffee cup from my hands and placed it on the floor. The butterflies were back in full force. I looked into his eyes, which were blue and clear and suddenly all I wanted was for him to kiss me.

He took my hands and I almost held my breath. The room disappeared and all that mattered was that he was sitting in front of me gently holding my hands. He leaned forward and his lips brushed mine. His hands cupped my face and as he was about to kiss me again, a loud ringing from my clutch broke the spell.

Hang up. Hang up, I thought frantically. You're ruining the moment, whoever you are. 'I don't need to get that,' I murmured, and thankfully the noise stopped. About a millisecond later it began again.

Alex sat back, with what looked like a slight smile on his face. 'Do you need to get that?'

I had played this moment over in my head *so* many times and now that it was actually happening, I couldn't believe that we were being interrupted by my phone. Reluctantly I reached for the clutch which I had tossed carelessly on the floor and picked out the offending object. Basils name was flashing angrily on the screen. What the hell did he want I thought angrily. I pressed answer and before I even had a chance to say 'hello', his angry voice yelled down the line.

'Where the fuck are you?' I've been looking everywhere for you. I know you're here.' He sounded deranged.

I held the phone away from my ear and glanced at Alex. He had raised his eyebrows and from his expression I assumed that he had heard Basil's outburst.

Taking a deep breath and making an effort to keep my voice civil I replied as calmly as I could manage. 'I'm at the Ferndale chambers party.' Not that it's any of your business where I am I thought sullenly.

'Where are you? In the fucking attic? I've looked everywhere for you.'

'Is there something I can help you with Basil?' Him screaming at me about where the fuck I was, wasn't progressing matters.

'Of course there bloody well is. I'm hardly ringing you in the middle of a party for a social chat am I? I got a call to say that Shane Reid has been arrested for Handling Stolen Goods. I spoke with the Officers and they said that he won't be interviewed before tomorrow. I want you to cover it in the morning.'

Typical Basil I thought. He didn't even have the courtesy to ask if I was available to cover it.

'I'm not sure that I can..,' I trailed off as Basil interrupted.

'Kate *make* yourself available. I'm not losing Shane

as a client because you won't attend for his interview. You know he will only deal with you. He's at Vauxhall Police Station.' He paused for a moment. 'Right I'll text you the details I have and I'll leave you to fucking cover it tomorrow so. Night.' He hung up before I could say anything else.

I couldn't believe it. I stared at my phone in amazement. On second thoughts I could. Basil had never really been civil to me, but his behaviour on that phone call had been downright obnoxious.

'Is he always so charming?' Alex asked breaking the stunned silence.

'What an asshole,' he added, to my delight.

'I know. He is the definition of an asshole,' I said getting great pleasure in openly calling Basil an asshole. It was nice to say the words aloud.

'Unfortunately Basil has ruined my seduction plan,' Alex joked.

My heart leapt. Alex had wanted to seduce me!

'So since you'll probably be spending the first half of the day at Vauxhall Police station, could I tempt you to spend tomorrow evening with me, having dinner?' Alex looked shyly at me.

Inside I was doing cartwheels. A date! Alex was asking me out on a date. Outwardly I smiled and said that that would be lovely.

'Shall we get you a cab m'lady?' he asked gesturing gallantly with his hand.

As I rode home that evening my thoughts weren't of the taxi fare that I really couldn't afford or of Basil's beyond rude phone call. I thought of how I felt when Alex's lips had brushed mine. It had felt amazing.

CHAPTER NINETEEN

A few hours later, my alarm sounded right beside my ear. When I'd stumbled into bed a little earlier, I must have thought that the only hope I would have of waking up was if the offending noise was right beside my eardrum. Without moving my body, my hand groped to turn it off. Silence.

Then I remembered. I had to go to the police station this morning. My body felt as though it didn't have an ounce of energy left to give. My eyes didn't want to open and the thought of getting out of bed seemed like a mammoth effort.

Suddenly the phone was ringing loudly in my ear again. This time it was a phone call. My head was throbbing and my throat felt raw.

'Hello,' I rasped.

'Oh I'm sorry I must have dialled the wrong number,' a chirpy voice said. 'I was looking for a Miss Hunter.'

'Miss Hunter speaking,' I croaked once more. I tried coughing to see if that would improve my ability to be heard.

'Oh Miss Hunter, I *am* sorry. This is PC Black. I understand that you will be the solicitor dealing with Mr. Reid today. We will be ready to interview him at 9am. Can you confirm that you will be able to attend at that time?'

While she had been speaking I had been pulling the sleep from the corners of my eyes so that I was now able to squint at the time on my phone. 7.30am. I had had three hours sleep.

'I'll be there,' I confirmed, sounding only marginally more alert.

I could go back to sleep for half an hour I mused but

I knew from experience that, that would just prolong the agony of having to get up. With a sudden decisiveness, I swung my legs over the bed and stood. A wave of dizziness swept over me. Bloody Shane Reid I muttered.

At 8.55, I walked up the steps to the station, clutching a Costa coffee cup in my hand. I had downed some Nurofen plus and I could feel my headache subsiding somewhat. The barista had asked if I wanted an extra shot, which is coffee shop speak for 'you look like crap and need waking up'. I didn't feel offended. I knew that I looked rough. I had asked for two extra shots. I needed all the help I could get.

As I waited in the lobby area, I sat in one of the ubiquitous blue metal chairs, drank my coffee and waited for the caffeine to hit my system. PC Black emerged 5 minutes later and was a ball of energy. She was petite and looked all of about twelve.

As she led me through to the custody suite, she chattered non-stop about everything from the weather to Christmas presents. She didn't seem to need any input from me other than the occasional nod. If I hadn't taken the Nurofen her voice would probably have tipped me over the edge.

After the formalities were carried out with the custody sergeant, I followed her into a consultation room. It was small and stuffy and wasn't going to help how I was feeling.

I decided to get the ball rolling.

'So, I understand that Shane was arrested last night for Handling Stolen Goods? What more can you tell me?' I questioned, my pen poised over my notebook to indicate that I just wanted to get on with this.

'I actually have typed disclosure if you'd find that easier?' she said sliding a page towards me.

'Great. Thanks,' I replied with enthusiasm.

I sat back to read the sheet.

'Shane Reid was arrested at 22.48 last night as he is suspected of Handling Stolen Goods. He was seen walking and acting in a suspicious manner on Clapham High Street. As he is known to the police, he was stopped and searched. His rucksack was also searched and it had a number of mobile phones, an I-pad and a laptop in it. These have previously been reported as stolen. He was arrested and made no comment on arrest.'

I digested this. I had no doubt that Shane had known the goods were stolen. It was his crime of choice and no matter how many times he said that he wanted to change his life, it seemed that he couldn't help himself. I didn't need to ask about Shane's list of previous convictions. I knew that it was lengthy and contained over thirty convictions for various offences. I also knew that Shane wouldn't be released on bail after today's interview. He would be charged with the offence of Handling Stolen Goods and remanded in police custody over the weekend. He would then appear before the courts on Monday morning to enter a plea to the charge.

I asked the officer to bring in Shane. Moments later a sheepish looking Shane walked into the room and sat down opposite me. He was 58, about 5 foot 8 inches tall with a pot belly. He wore glasses which today had sellotape circled around the nosepiece. He certainly didn't look like the average person who spent their lives in and out of jail.

'Kate you never let me down. You're always there for me,' he began. Shane was one of those clients who thought we were genuinely friends.

'Well Shane, as your solicitor I have your best interests at heart.' No point in telling him that the only reason I was here at all, was because Basil had pretty much ordered me to represent him.

'So Shane, what can you tell me about the goods they found on you?' I said keen to get the show on the road.

Shane blushed which was unusual for him. He was generally very chatty. He almost seemed embarrassed.

'I know I said I was going to change things Kate, but I just can't help myself. I'm sorry,' he said, avoiding eye contact with me at all times.

'Shane,' I said gently. 'I'm only here to advise you. I'm not going to judge you. Now can you tell me what happened?'

'I know Kate. It's just that I was trying to be good. I was even writing you letters to try and stay straight. Did you get them?' he asked looking at me hopefully.

'Yes Shane, I got them.' I didn't add that I couldn't understand how writing two line letters to me was going to keep him on the straight and narrow. I wanted to try and get him to focus on why he was in police custody.

'Shane, we really need to talk about the items they found on you, when they stopped you in Clapham. The fact that you live in Stoke Newington is going to make the officers wonder why you were down in Clapham, with the items that were reported stolen.'

Once again he blushed furiously. I couldn't understand what was wrong with him. I wasn't oblivious to the fact that he had some sort of infatuation with me. The letters he had sent were proof of that. But he had never acted so strangely around me before.

'Kate, I knew the goods were stolen. I'm going to go 'no comment' in the interview and they will charge me. Then I'll be remanded until Monday morning for court.' He said all this in a very matter of fact way.

I smiled at him. 'Well Shane, at least you don't have any delusions about walking out of here today.' He smiled back at me.

'So Kate, what are you doing for the rest of the weekend?' Once again he was trying to act like a friend.

'Oh, you know. This and that,' I said in an off-hand way. 'Ok Shane you stay here and I'll go and get the officers.' I was eager to prevent any personal chat. Even though I was only stepping outside the door and signalling to the officers who were standing down the corridor, I took my handbag with me. Despite us being on the client's side they were still expert criminals and I didn't trust Shane not to pick something from my bag.

About an hour later I was leaving the station and my only thoughts were of crawling back into bed. I decided to text Basil that I had done his bidding. I pulled my phone out of my bag. There was a text from Alex.

I hope you've escaped Vauxhall PS and are in the mood for some Spanish fare? How about Barrafina in Soho at 8? Maybe turn off your phone so we're not interrupted!

I smiled and quickly replied:

Sounds great. I'm looking forward to it'

It was mid-day. I was sure that after a powernap I would feel refreshed and ready for my date. I sent Basil a quick text.

Finished at VPS. No result yet but will be charged and remanded for certain. I can cover Monday court

At least this would mean I was putting off having to see Basil. After his demanding phone call last night I wasn't in any hurry to see his large frame or hear his irritating voice.

Fast forward eight hours and I was feeling remarkably better. It's amazing what a few hours sleep can do for a person. I felt part of the human race again and not just a zombie who was only functioning because I had consumed huge quantities of caffeine.

'No. Really?' Alex spluttered, as I finished telling a story about Basil and more of his outrageous behaviour. I felt fun and flirty as we sat close together at the tapas bar. I had been afraid of awkward moments but everything was easy and natural. Laura would be delighted. I was on a proper date with a normal guy and I was acting like myself.

After we had realised that we were the last ones left in the restaurant, we moved onto a late night bar and sat cosily in the corner drinking more wine. It seemed natural to hold his hand and when he asked if he could take me out on a second date I answered him with a kiss. I was well and truly smitten. Later when he hailed me a cab, I was reluctant to leave.

'I really enjoyed tonight Kate. We can have a lot of fun when Basil is kept out of the equation,' he smiled winking at me.

I grinned back at him.

'Well are ya gettin' in or what?' the cabbie asked grumpily.

As I was about to dive into the taxi, Alex brushed his lips against mine. The butterflies in my stomach went into overdrive. I felt like I could kiss him all night. He smiled at me as the cab pulled away and I spent the entire journey grinning. As I was climbing into bed a little later I got a text from him. It simply read;

Xx

Just perfect I thought.

CHAPTER TWENTY

Monday morning found me in Camberwell Green Magistrates Court which was my least favourite courthouse. It was dull, dreary and seemed to operate at its own pace.

At ten am the prosecutor still hadn't arrived with the papers for Shane. I decided to occupy myself by playing Tetris on my phone. At 10.20 I took another look into the courtroom but there was still no sign of a prosecutor. What was especially annoying was that the courts were constantly talking of 'speedy justice'. The aim of this was to get cases dealt with as quickly as possible. It was obviously not working at its best this morning. Just as I was about to leave, a list caller emerged from the door beside the bench. Progress!

Her sizeable frame waddled towards me and she gave me a beaming smile, which was infectious. Someone had gotten the week off to a good start.

'Morning,' I couldn't help but smile back at her. 'I'm representing Shane Reid. I'm Miss Hunter. Do you happen to have any idea where the prosecutor is?' I asked hopefully.

'Childcare issues Miss,' she said as she wrote my name next to Shanes.

'Any idea when he or she is expected to arrive?'

'Apparently she's arrived and is upstairs gathering today's files so hopefully not too long more.'

Just then a harried and flustered looking woman scurried into the courtroom, hauling a cart with all the Prosecution files. She looked like she was having a disaster of a morning. Her shirt was hanging out over her black trousers and due to her lack of a suit jacket I could see sweat patches had already formed under her arms. Her diminutive frame began lifting heavy files from the cart and placing them on her bench. I could see she was trying to get some semblance of calm into her morning by placing them in alphabetical order. When she eventually finished this, she began groping around in her handbag. She produced a packet of Nurofen and popped a couple in her mouth. Only then did she seem to take a breath.

I stood staring at her, trying to gauge when it might be safe to approach and ask for Shane's papers. I had a feeling that she might snarl at me. Behind me defence lawyers were beginning to gather, all looking for something from the Prosecutor.

After I had done the obligatory eye-rolling and knowing smiles with some of the other defence advocates I moved towards her.

'Good morning,' I began.

'Is it?' she replied. 'I hadn't noticed,' she said eyeing the jostling line of lawyers behind me, as she tried to pull her unruly hair into a bun.

Deciding that now wasn't the time for pleasantries I asked her directly for Shane's papers.

'Won't be ready until after lunch.' Evidently she was finished talking to me, as she was already looking behind me at the short stubby man who was engrossed in his I-pad.

'Can I help you?' she asked him curtly.

'Ooh sorry,' he chortled. Got caught up in this. Did you know.....' he trailed off as he saw the scowl on her face and blushed a deep scarlet. For a tiny woman she definitely had a presence.

I had over 3 hours until I would get the papers and Shane was my only client so I couldn't occupy myself with someone else. There was no point in travelling back to the office. I decided that I might as well go and get instructions from Shane. I pretty much knew what the papers would say anyway, as I had been with him in interview.

Down in the cells, I waited for about twenty minutes for a consultation room to become available. I listened to the banter back and forth between the custody officers. It mainly revolved around whatever they had read in the Sun that day or whatever football match was coming up.

When a room was free, I tucked my handbag into a shelf, as we weren't allowed to bring these into consultation with clients. I suppose in case we passed something to them or allowed them to make a call from our mobiles. I knew that this wasn't beyond the scope of possibilities. Clients were so fickle that some lawyers would often cross over the line, just to keep them on side.

As I sat waiting for Shane, I began filling out the 14 page legal aid form which needed to be completed and submitted to the legal aid board so as my firm could get paid for representing him. I knew without a doubt, given Shanes lengthy list of previous convictions and the fact that a custodial sentence was highly likely that we would get legal aid for him.

Shane had a goofy look on his face when he walked in and looked to be in good spirits for someone who had spent two nights at Vauxhall Police Station.

'Morning Shane, how are you doing? How was Vauxhalls hospitality?'

'Morning Kate,' he said sounding in good spirits.

'Well the food was tasteless as usual and the bedding could be more comfortable but other than that I've got no complaints.' For someone who had spent the weekend in police custody he was remarkably happy.

'Shane, the Prosecutor doesn't have papers for you yet. We might as well discuss how you want to proceed today and complete the legal aid forms,' I said tapping the papers in front of me with my pen.'

'So, do you want to tell me more about where you got the items you were arrested with?'

'I was given 'em by a mate Kate. He asked me to hold onto 'em for a while.'

'Where were you going to keep them Shane?'

'At mine.'

'Did you know or believe that they were stolen goods?'

''Course Kate. That mate's about as straight as a bent wire.'

I smiled at the simple analogy.

'Was there any particular reason why you said you would hold onto them? Were you pressurised into doing it?'

'We do things like that for each other Kate. I know it's not right but that's how we do things. He would help me out another time.'

'Okay Shane, well it's going to be a guilty plea, but you'll get full credit for that. Next we need to discuss the possible sentence. I can ask the judge to consider getting a Pre Sentence report if you would like some input from the Probation Services?'

'Well it's worth a shot Kate but with my record I'd say I'm goin' to be goin' away for a while today.'

'If he does order a report Shane how about we go for it altogether and make a bail application?'

'Sure, why not Kate,' he said with a wide grin. He knew that his chance of getting bail today was slim.

We discussed for a little while what conditions I could put forward to the Judge if I had to make a bail application. Predictably he said that to get bail he would comply with any conditions the Judge wanted to put in place. After signing the legal aid forms I left the custody suite and checked the time. I guess it was time for an early lunch.

Our case was finally called on at 3.30 that afternoon. When Shane was bought up from the cells, I could see that he was agitated. The charge was put to him and a guilty plea was entered. The court then went on to decide what to do about sentence.

Amazingly the Judge decided to order a Pre Sentence Report before sentencing Shane. He raised his eyebrows when I said I would be making a bail application. Up hill battle here Kate I thought.

After talking at length about why Shane should be granted bail, I summed up by saying that he would comply with any stringent conditions the court felt necessary to put in place.

As I sat down, I waited for the Judge to deny bail. His head was bowed and he was writing notes. After a long wait, he eventually spoke and amazingly granted Shane bail. I actually couldn't believe it. Basil would be delighted. The next case was called on and I left the courtroom, bowing slightly at the Judge before I exited. I walked down to the sub ground level where the cells were, fully expecting a jubilant Shane. He was led into a consultation room by a detention officer. He didn't look as thrilled as I thought he would be. There's just no pleasing some people.

'Ok Shane, so I'll just run through the conditions you will have to comply with. Firstly you must report to Stoke Newington Police station every Monday, Wednesday and Friday between the hours of 2pm and 4pm. Secondly you must attend any appointments Probation make for you. Thirdly you must abide by a tagged curfew between the hours of 8pm and 7am and finally you must not enter the borough of Lambeth.'

I looked up from my notes to look at Shane. He looked dispirited.

'Shane what's the matter? I thought you would be delighted?'

'I am Kate but I can't go to Lambeth now as it's one of my conditions.'

I didn't get it. How would this so adversely affect Shane.

'But Shane you live in Stoke Newington. Why do you so desperately need to go to the borough of Lambeth.'

'I need to go to Clapham sometimes Kate.' He looked agitated again.

'Is that where your friend who gave you the stuff lives?'

Shane nodded.

'Well you're probably better off staying away from him for a while Shane.' I tried not to lecture clients, so stopped myself there. It wasn't my place to tell them what to do. It was my job to advise and represent them as best I could.

'There's a girl I like who lives in Clapham. I was leaving presents for her. Now I won't be able to do it anymore,' he said dejectedly.

Ah, so Shane had a crush.

'Well Shane I'm afraid she'll have to wait until the bail conditions are lifted for her next present. I'm sure she will understand.'

'But she doesn't know it's me.'

I stopped gathering my things as a thought occurred to me. I glanced up at Shane who was looking down at his hands which were clasped on the table in front of us. No, don't be silly Kate, I told myself, shaking my head to banish the thought.

'Okay, Shane, you'll be out of here shortly. Be good and I'll see you for your sentencing hearing in three weeks,' I said as I stood and backed towards the door. Suddenly I just wanted to be out of this claustrophobic stale air.

As I walked to the bus, I considered the ridiculous

thought which had entered my mind in the cells with Shane. Surely the roses hadn't been from him? I shuddered at the thought. There was no way he could have figured out where I lived. Was there?

After mulling over various scenarios on the bus journey back to the office, I decided that I was being paranoid. I didn't have any basis for thinking that the roses were from Shane. Talk about being melodramatic Kate, I said sternly to myself.

CHAPTER TWENTY ONE

Later that afternoon, I was back at the office trying to make inroads into my paperwork, when Nick barged into the office. He was fizzing with energy.

'I *am* the man,' he stated triumphantly his hands raised above his head. 'Just got acquitted on five charges of Harassment. I *am* the man!' he repeated, as he collapsed into his chair.

I smiled looking up at him. I could understand his jubilation. Getting acquitted on a charge at trial was a wonderful feeling. It definitely put a spring into your step for the rest of the day.

'Was that the Hamza trial?'

Hamza was a regular client of ours who had a penchant for beating up his wife. In fact he saw it as his God given right to beat her up. He viewed her as his property. She had eventually gone to court to get a Restraining order against him. However he had almost made breaching it his hobby. No doubt Nick would be representing him again soon, very possibly for the exact same reason.

'Yep. He was totally guilty but the wife just crumbled on the stand. She was in floods of tears and got her story so mixed up that it made it easy to discredit her.'

I hated those cross-examinations. You had to represent your client to the best of your ability but it often meant that you had to really push the person you were questioning. Sometimes, particularly in very sensitive cases the person being questioned broke down crying. I usually hated myself a little after those types of trials.

'Fancy a coffee? I feel knackered after today and need a caffeine hit,' Nick asked.

'When do I not want a coffee? Kitchen coffee or Starbucks?'

'The good stuff. Let's do Starbucks,' he said standing. 'I feel like I deserve a treat after today.'

'So was Hamza released then today?' I questioned, as we walked out of the office.

'No. He's serving a sentence for ABH. He's due to be released in two weeks though so I'd imagine his first stop will be his wife's, so as he can vent his frustration at having to go through today's trial. I'm sure I'll be seeing him at the Police station then.'

'That's if his wife has any courage left after today's trial to phone the police. I'm sure she won't want to go through today all over again,' I said.

'Hey don't you start getting all self righteous on me!' he said with a grin, as he held the door to Starbucks open. The soothing aroma of coffee hit me.

'What would you like? I asked. 'My treat. As a well done gift for winning today.'

' Ooh in that case I'll have a Venti hot chocolate and a chocolate brownie.'

'Is that your new code for a black Americano?' Nick was so predictable when it came to coffee. He never indulged in any of the syrups, whipped creams or sprinkles that Starbucks had to offer.

'Am I that boring?'

'Afraid so,' I said smiling as I walked towards the counter.

Once we were settled at a table by the window Nick asked me what I had been up to today at court.

'My favourite client Shane Reid, was in for Handling Stolen Goods. Actually I should be celebrating too. I managed to convince Judge Cannon that a presentence report should be obtained before sentence *and* the best part is he was released on bail.'

Nick frowned.

'What's the matter? That's a really good result,' I said a bit peeved that Nick didn't seem to share my delight.

'I really don't think it's right that you continue representing him Kate. We all know that his feelings for you go beyond the normal client/lawyer adoration. Also those letters he was sending you....it just seems inappropriate that's all. I'll gladly take him on as a client for you?'

I weighed up telling Nick about what had occurred to me while I was in the cells with Shane. I figured I had nothing to lose.

'When I got him bail today, I thought he would be ecstatic. I mean he *should* have been,...' I trailed off. Was I just being absolutely ridiculous?

'Go on,' Nick said encouragingly.

'I'm probably just being silly and reading into something which isn't even there but...'

'But what Kate?'

'Ok, you'll probably think I'm stupid but one of his bail conditions is that he can't go to the borough of Lambeth. He was found with the stolen goods in Clapham,' I said by way of explanation.

'When I went to see him in the cells after the hearing, he seemed almost annoyed about the condition.'

'But doesn't he live in North London?' Nick interjected.

'Yes, that's why I thought it was odd that he was so irritated by it. But then he said that he was leaving gifts for a girl he fancied in Clapham and that because of the bail condition he wouldn't be able to do this anymore. He also said the girl didn't know that it was him leaving the gifts.' I stalled because Nick was looking very puzzled.

'I don't get what this has to do with how he is with

159

you?'

'The thing is, remember the roses I thought you had left for me? Well it was just the way he looked at me when we were in the cell that really creeped me out and made me wonder if it was him leaving me the roses?'

Nick was just staring at me.

'I know. It's completely ludicrous isn't it?' I said hurriedly.

Still Nick didn't say anything. After a long pause he spoke.

'No actually I don't think you're being silly Kate. In fact I think you need to cease acting for him from now.'

'I would straight away if it wasn't for Basil.' I recounted the phone call I had had from Basil on Friday night.

Nick looked aghast. 'I can't believe he spoke to you like that Kate.'

'I'm pretty used to it Nick,' I said with resignation. He treats us girls a lot differently to how he treats the guys. I know if I even broach the subject with him, he'll probably burst a blood vessel and start popping those pills he always carries about.'

'Something just doesn't seem right about it all Kate. Are you sure I can't convince you to ask Basil to allow someone else to represent him?'

'Not at the moment Nick. It could just be my overactive imagination and I really can't afford to push Basils buttons at the moment.'

'Just promise me that you'll keep me updated if anything else happens?'

'I promise Nick,' I said as I slurped back the last of my coffee.

CHAPTER TWENTY TWO

Later that night, I sat on the couch staring at my phone which lay silent and unmoving on the coffee table. My on call shift had started an hour ago but annoyingly I hadn't had any calls yet.

'Come on people. Start getting drunk, having fights, or whatever,' I muttered to myself. Tonight was my last night of being duty solicitor before Christmas. It was my chance to earn some extra money and I had been expecting it to be a busy night. People would no doubt be stealing Christmas gifts, getting too drunk at the Christmas party, beating up their girlfriends and committing various other crimes which came hand and hand with the festive period. But nothing so far.

Suddenly my phone beeped. Disappointingly it was only a text. I leaned forward to get the phone and my heart did a little flutter when I saw that it was from Alex.

So have you picked up anyone who you will be representing at Westminster tomorrow? I'm there all day and would love a coffee date?

I'm sure I had a big goofy grin on my face. We had been texting back and forth since our date on Saturday night and I was more smitten than ever. Oh I really hoped that I represented someone tonight who was remanded for court tomorrow morning.

While I tried to think up some witty fun response, I went back to flicking through the magazine which lay on my lap. Unable to think of anything funny to say I resorted to simply answering his question.

All quiet so far. I would love a coffee date too, especially if you throw in some chocolate cake!

A reply pinged back almost immediately.

If that's what it takes to get you to come!

I blushed and was glad that I was on my own. I knew what he had meant but it made me think of running my hands down his naked chest as he undid my bra, his hands making me hot with desire.

I was engrossed in my daydream when the phone started ringing loudly. I always put it on the loudest volume setting when I was on call. Just in case I missed it ringing and would be responsible for Basil having some sort of apoplectic fit. I sighed reluctant to break out of my fantasy.

'Hello, Miss Hunter speaking.'

'Good evening Miss Hunter,' a pleasant Geordie accent said. 'This is the Defence Solicitors Call Centre. Are you available to take a call?'

'Hi, yes I am,' I confirmed. I grabbed the pen and paper I had on the coffee table so as I could take down the details.

'We have an adult male arrested for domestic assault at Charing Cross Police Station.' She continued to give me the other relevant details and the case number.

After I had hung up, I phoned up the station to find out about the status of the case and whether they would be interviewing tonight or in the morning. I spoke to the Officer in the Case and was informed that they were hoping the interview would take place at 2am that morning. After chatting briefly with the client I was assured that he was very relaxed about being at the station. I warned him not to speak to the police about his case until I got to Charing Cross but from his easy going attitude I assumed that he was a regular in custody suites and wouldn't be doing this anyway.

I checked the time once I was finished speaking with him. It was 11.30. I could try and get an hour and a half sleep I supposed. Although the chances of me actually falling asleep were slim. Unfortunately I wasn't one of those people who could nod off easily.

I decided to catch up on some episodes of 'The Good Wife', which I had recorded. I would just have to put up with being absolutely wrecked tomorrow. Sitting back, I wrapped myself in a blanket and dissolved into the glamorous world of law in America. Programmes like this were probably partly responsible for getting me to go into law. Someone really ought to write a series about what it's *actually* like to work in the English courts.

At 1.15am I reluctantly peeled myself off the couch, gathered my papers and headed out into the bitter cold. I really hoped that the officers would be ready to go when I got to the station. I wasn't in the mood for hanging around an icy cold reception area. As I was driving I got another call about a client who was in West End Central station. I pulled over to take down the details and was told that the client was extremely intoxicated and wouldn't be fit for interview until the morning. The poor guy. There was a good chance that he would wake up tomorrow, completely confused by his surroundings and wondering why the hell he was in a police cell. It happened all the time. Being hungover in a police cell must be an awful feeling.

After parking the car about a mile from the station, I walked briskly to keep warm and once inside phoned through to the custody suite. Typically the officers took about twenty minutes to come and save me from the drunk and homeless looking man who I assumed was hiding out from the freezing weather. He kept moving too close to me for comfort and was ranting in a nonsensical manner. After a while I gave up smiling politely at him and tried scowling instead. Unfortunately it didn't seem to deter him.

Eventually the officers arrived and I jumped gratefully to my feet. As we walked through to the custody centre the homeless man shouted after me, 'I see your soul. I see your soul.'

I rolled my eyes.

CHAPTER TWENTY-THREE

Many hours later, I walked bleary eyed out of the station. After my arrival, the officers had decided to go and do a s18 search of his home, which had meant I had spent over an hour trying to better my top score in Tetris. I hadn't. After their search had revealed a grand total of nothing, they then decided to interview him. It was 4.30 am, I was exhausted and had to be up at 7am for court. The client had been charged with ABH and had been remanded and would appear at Westminster Magistrates Court in a few hours time. The silver lining was that I would get that coffee date with Alex. Once again he would get the overly tired version of me.

The only benefit of being out on call at this hour was the light traffic so I was home in under a half an hour. I really hoped that the speeding cameras hadn't been working. As I walked up our driveway wondering if I'd be able to get two hours sleep, I froze.

Lying on the doorstep, was a single red rose, with the by now familiar white card attached. I groped around for my key, cursing my big bag. I just wanted to be on the other side of the front door as quickly as possible. Finding it, and with a shaky hand, I scooped up the rose and threw my body weight against the door as I jiggled the key in the lock. Once inside, I locked and bolted the door. I wished Laura was here, but she wasn't going to be back until later this evening.

The hallway was flooded with light as I flicked the switch. I sat on the stairs, all thoughts of sleep forgotten and read the card. It looked exactly like the others and the scrawl was the same. This time it read;

'Nothing will keep us from seeing each other Kate'
xxx

I felt vulnerable, scared and alone. I had nothing

which I could use to prove that it was Shane who was leaving the roses. In fact all I had to go on was gut feeling. Or maybe I was just overreacting because I was exhausted? A thought occurred to me. Every time a rose had been placed on the doorstep, I had been out of the house. Was the person who was leaving the flowers watching my movements? The thought freaked me out and terrified me in equal measures. I knew that one of Shanes bail conditions was that he wasn't to enter Clapham. However I wasn't so naive that I didn't think he was beyond breaking this condition. Many clients saw their bail conditions as something they had to adhere to until they became an inconvenience. Shane wasn't any different. I had represented him numerous times for breach of his bail conditions.

There was no way I was going to be able to sleep now, so I headed into the kitchen and put the kettle on. Coffee probably wasn't the best thing to drink now as I was so agitated but my body was crying out for it. Maybe one of my new year's resolutions should be to cut down on my caffeine intake, I mused. I doubted this would ever happen.

Moments later I clutched my coffee mug in both hands and sat on the couch in the sitting room. I was deep in thought. Eventually after formulating a plan of action I felt somewhat better and I was glad when it was 7.15 and time for me to get ready to meet the day ahead. I sent a quick text to Basil about the client in West End Central Station and told him that I would be at Westminster today covering an overnighter. After a shower and some breakfast the fear I had been feeling a couple of hours earlier had dissipated somewhat and I knew how I was going to tackle this. Also Laura was coming home tonight so I wouldn't be alone in the house anymore which was a relief.

Hours later, at City of Westminster Magistrates Court, I was still waiting for papers for my overnight client. I had suspected that this would happen as his interview had only taken place a few hours ago. I pulled out my phone and sent a text to Alex.

I'm slowly losing the will to live. No papers (surprise surprise!) Think I'm in need of a coffee hit! Fancy being my accomplice?

A reply pinged back almost immediately, so I didn't have time to consider whether using the word 'accomplice' was just nerdy.

There must be paper shortages in the CPS-I don't have any either. Plus side we get our coffee date. See you at the front door in five

I ducked into the ladies and looked at myself in the mirror. My undereye circles were a reminder that I hadn't had any sleep. Momentarily I thought again of the roses but I shook my head to clear out the thoughts. I was going to ask Basil to remove Shane from my client list and hopefully that would put a stop to the 'gifts'. I put on another coat of mascara and applied some lipgloss although it didn't really do anything to hide my exhausted face.

As I walked towards the front door I thought of Alex's text to me last night. Just thinking about it made me all tingly. I could make out his physique as I neared the front door. He was on his phone pacing up and down. My heart began to beat a little faster. The fact that I could be waiting here for papers until the late afternoon no longer seemed to matter. As I got closer he hung up and turned to face me. I saw two female barristers eyeing him out of the corner of my eye. I couldn't blame them. He was *so* handsome.

'Miss Hunter,' he said with a grin. 'I'm glad the CPS are particularly inefficient today as we get to have coffee together.'

'Alex, hi,' I smiled goofily at him. 'If ever there was someone in need of coffee it's me right now.'

'Late night?' he asked, stepping aside so as I could pass through the doors first. As I walked past I could smell the aftershave he used. I had begun to associate this smell with Alex. So much so that even on the tube if I smelt it on a guy my mind immediately thought of him.

'Well it would have been late if I had made it to bed. One of these days Alex, you'll catch me on a day when I've had some sleep.'

'Were you at a police station? Where do you fancy for coffee by the way? Shall we walk towards Baker Street and maybe go to Costa?'

'Yep, that sounds perfect. I was at Charing Cross Police station with my overnighter. By the time I'm finished with him today, I'll have chatted to him more than I've spoken to my sister in the last month!'

'Tell me about it,' Alex groaned. Remember that youth robbery trial I was telling you about?'

'Yes, the 5 hander?' I asked as I pulled my scarf tighter around my neck. The tiredness was making me feel the cold even more.

'Well, at the end of that I felt like I should be inviting the kid around for dinner. Right what's your coffee preference? An extra shot?' he asked as we walked into the cosy warmth of Costa.

'Please.' I said gratefully. As I looked for a table, I rubbed my left eye to try and get it to stop twitching. Annoyingly it did this at the most inappropriate of times and it was usually because I was exhausted. I found a table downstairs in the corner and plopped myself down in the brown leather couch.

Alex sat down a few minutes later, placing two coffees and a chocolate tiffin slice on the table. 'You looked like you could do with a sugar rush,' he said explaining the chocolate slice. 'Although it may have more to do with my sweet tooth,' he said somewhat sheepishly.

After a few moments of comfortable silence, where I tried to get as much caffeine into my system as quickly as possible Alex interrupted my mission.

'So Kate,' he said sounding somewhat hesitant, which was strange when he always seemed so self assured.

'Em, so, I don't know if you would be interested, or even free,' he said hurriedly, the words falling from his mouth.

I looked at him, waiting for him to continue, curious about what had got him so flustered.

'Well, you see, my Dad has an annual Christmas party at the house where he invites around his cronies and well I was wondering if you'd like to go with me this year?' He seemed relieved that he'd gotten the words out. Now he was looking at me expectantly. I certainly hadn't anticipated that!

'Oh,' he added, remembering that he hadn't told me when it was on. 'It's on the day before Christmas Eve?'

I had been planning on going home that day for Christmas but I definitely didn't want to miss this party so I quickly decided that I'd go home on Christmas Eve instead.

'I'd love to go,' I said simply.

Alex looked relieved and I couldn't help grinning at him. He started talking about another chambers Christmas party he had been at recently and about a certain married QC who was notorious for trying it on with the youngest female members of the chambers. This year his target had been a very attractive girl who was well able to take care of herself. Unlike his usual conquests who complied with his warning not to tell anyone about his indiscretions this girl had broadcast his futile attempts at wooing her to anyone who would listen. Apparently the QC's wife had heard about it on the grapevine and had unceremoniously thrown him out of their house. As he talked on I wondered excitedly what I would wear to his parents party. As I was mentally going through my wardrobe Alex announced that we should be getting back to court.

Suddenly a wave of tiredness swept over me and my eye started twitching again. Damn it I thought.

'I can't believe how much 'out of hours' work you solicitors have to do,' Alex said sympathetically. I obviously wasn't doing a very good job of hiding how tired I was.

'Although with the way things are going at the Bar, I know that a few of my Colleagues are thinking of becoming 'Duty qualified' so as they can earn some extra money from police station attendances.'

'I know, the way our profession is going really worries me,' I said tiredly

Obviously realising that I wasn't in the mood for a 'state of our profession' discussion Alex asked if I'd like another coffee to go.

I shook my head. I was already beginning to feel a little jittery after the amount I had already consumed today. Being tired, emotional and jittery wasn't a good look at court, particularly when you were trying to put forward someone's best case. It was sometimes easy to forget that what was an earth shattering calamity for a client is just another day in the office for me.

As we walked back to the courthouse, Alex suddenly stopped walking and turned towards me. Momentarily I thought he was going to kiss me and my heart leapt. Instead he took my glove covered hands in his.

'Kate you really need to take care of yourself. I

don't like seeing you this exhausted. I know Basil is difficult to deal with but there must be some way that you can avoid having to do so much out of hours work? Also the benefit for me would be that I'd get to take you on a second 'proper' date,' he added with a grin.

Now wasn't the time to tell him that, as I didn't live at home like many of my colleagues did and didn't have an income from my parents some others benefited from I had to scrounge around for as many out of hour's attendances as I could.

'Maybe you're right,' I said with resignation. I *knew* he was right but at the moment I couldn't see any other way. I needed money to pay rent, bills, my huge student loan and generally to live. As I couldn't do this on my salary I *needed* do the 'out of hours' work.

'I'm sure I'll feel rejuvenated after Christmas,' I added with a smile.

'Right let's see if they have some papers for us,' Alex declared, as we entered the courthouse.

CHAPTER TWENTY FOUR

Hours later, I trudged wearily down the stairs of the courthouse. I felt beaten by the system. The papers for my client had never arrived and the Judge had forced me to make a spur of the moment bail application as he had refused to delay the case any longer. After a hurried whispered conversation with the client through the glass of the courtroom dock, I put forward his case for being granted bail until the next morning when hopefully the Crown would have his papers and his case could proceed. The Judge took all of two seconds to refuse the application so my client was being remanded over night because of the inefficiency of the CPS.

I wanted nothing more than to curl up in my bed and fall asleep for a couple of days. I realised I was running on empty but didn't see anything that I could do about it. I had a client appointment at five so there was no avoiding going back to the office.

About forty minutes later, I was back in the office feeling slightly better as I gripped my tea in my hands. I had decided that anymore coffee would possibly result in me having some sort of caffeine induced seizure in front of my next client. I checked my diary on the computer to remind myself who the meeting was with, but all that was written was 'client meeting'. Odd I thought. Usually the receptionist was very good at getting client details before they were actually sitting in front of us.

Suddenly there was a knock on the door.

'Come in,' I said loudly, holding back a sigh. A Client consultation after a night of no sleep and a day like today in court was definitely not what I wanted to be doing.

I stood and plastered a smile on my face, wondering who was going to emerge from behind the door.

I almost let the tea mug fall from my grip.

Shane Reid appeared. I took a deep breath and tried to compose myself.

He made his way towards the seat opposite my desk and sat down. I did the same, grateful for the support of the chair.

'Shane, hi, what can I do for you today?' I enquired, trying to prevent my voice from wobbling. Perhaps I was being overly emotional due to lack of sleep. I had conjured up a scenario in my head where Shane was a dangerous Psycho client, when really he had only ever been goofy and slightly dim when I had been dealing with him. Was I being overly dramatic?

Shane appeared agitated.

'Kate, 'member I was saying to you that the bail condition not to enter Lambeth was going to be tough for me to do?'

I held my breath waiting for him to continue.

'Well I need to get that condition removed. I can't do it.'

'But Shane, you know that getting bail in the first instance was nothing short of a miracle, particularly with your previous convictions and Failing to Surrenders on your record. Also you were found in Clapham with the stolen items so, as you know, it's standard practice for the court to put a ban on entering the place where the offence was committed.'

Shane looked at me straight in the eye which was unusual for him. He generally avoided eye contact and preferred to stare at his shoes or the floor when he was talking.

'Kate, I need it removed. You're my solicitor. You're supposed to act on my instructions.'

I had to make a big effort to hide the surprise from

my face. Shane had never spoken so forcefully to me before. This change in him was really freaking me out.

'I can get it listed Shane but I'll need a reason to tell the court why you can't comply with it. What *is* the reason?' I asked curiously.

'It's like I told you Kate, the girl I like is living in Clapham. The court would understand that, wouldn't they?'

'Well you would need to give me more details about this girl, such as, how long have you known her, what type of relationship do you have with her and whether or not it would be possible to meet her outside of Lambeth?' I felt anxious as I waited for his reply. I could have asked him if he had breached this condition already, such as last night, but as his solicitor I didn't want to know the answer.

'She lives in Clapham. What more do you want to know?' Shane said stubbornly.

'Shane the application will have a greater chance of success if I have as much detail as possible to tell the court.'

'Just forget it then Kate, alright? Just forget it,' he said aggressively. I had never seen this side of him before and I was really wishing that Nick would come back from wherever he was. I was beginning to feel very uncomfortable being alone in the room with him.

Shane stood, pushing back his chair with force.

'You're turning out to be just like everyone else. You just don't care at all do you?'

'Shane...' I broke off as he turned and stormed out of the office.

What the hell had that being about? My overly tired brain began trying to make sense of it all. Could my earlier theory about Shane and the roses have been right? Or was I simply over-reacting? I felt more confused than ever.

Making a decision, I went into my outlook and began typing an email to Basil. I really didn't care if it would piss him off. I felt that the time had come to pass on Shane to Nick. After clicking send, I checked the time. I could either wait around to see if Basil responded or I could make a break for it.

Standing, I grabbed my coat and scarf. I just wanted to be out of the office and at home quickly as possible.

CHAPTER TWENTY FIVE

About two hours later, thanks to tube delays, I was throwing myself against our front door. As I fell into the hallway, I felt a wave of relief wash over me. I knew Laura was home. Although the bags dumped at the foot of the stairs were a dead giveaway, I could smell something delicious wafting from the kitchen. Suddenly I didn't feel so alone anymore.

Just then Laura emerged from the kitchen, looking like a domestic goddess. She was wearing an apron, and was holding a spatula in her hand.

'Kate!' she shrieked, as she ran towards me. I smiled as she engulfed me. It felt so good to be hugged. As we untangled ourselves, Kate suddenly took off back towards the kitchen.

'I don't want the seabass to burn,' she called over her shoulder.

'Kate, what happened to you in Bali!' I joked. 'I didn't even know that you owned an apron and I've *never* seen you cook!'

'Do you like it?' she asked twirling and holding out the apron to show it off. 'It was handmade in Bali. I bought it in a little village there. Oh Kate the trip was *so amazing*,' she said sighing, lost in memories of her last ten days. She was looking tanned, relaxed and seemed to have her energetic spirit back.

'I can't wait to hear all about it, but first I need to get out of this suit.'

'Dinner should be ready in about 15 minutes,' Laura sing-songed after me as I climbed the stairs. I felt utterly exhausted and my bed looked so enticing. I longed to collapse into it and fall into a deep sleep for a couple of days. Just to take a break from the world for a while.

My stomach growled, telling me that it needed feeding before I could contemplate going to bed. A home cooked meal was a real treat, even if it had the potential to give me food poisoning as in all the years that I had known Laura, I think the most I had ever seen her do in the kitchen was make a cup of tea and unwrap a takeaway!

I followed the delicious smell downstairs and into the sitting room.

'How has ten days in Bali turned you into a culinary whizz?' I asked half jokingly but also half out of curiosity.' Not that I'm complaining,' I added hastily. I couldn't remember the last time I'd had a home cooked meal. Actually it was probably the last time I had been at home which was ....When *was* the last time I had made a visit home. I had been a seriously bad daughter this year. I resolved to make a big effort this Christmas. I had struck lucky with the duty rota and had four full days off over Christmas and I *couldn't wait.*

'You haven't tasted it yet,' Laura said somewhat anxiously.

'Well if it tastes as good as it smells it's going to be delicious,' I said as I settled onto the couch.

'So have you been working all the hours available?' Laura asked as she began to dish out the food. 'You look absolutely shattered Kate,' she said pausing momentarily to look me in the eyes.

'Oh you know, the usual,' I said hoping I sounded perky. I was too exhausted to begin talking about how tired I was.

Laura must have sensed that I wasn't in the mood for this particular discussion because she passed me a plate with a flourish.

'Bon appetite!' we both exclaimed at the same time. It was a habit of ours and I had no idea how it had started as neither of us had any French ties.

After the initial edge had been taken from our hunger and we had oohed and aahed over the food sufficiently, we began to catch up on what had happened over the past ten days.

After about an hour of sharing stories, squealing and lots of 'I can't believe its', my eyelids were beginning to droop and my left eye began twitching again. Recognising this as a sign that I was about to nod off mid sentence in front of her, Laura stood, gathered the dishes quickly and began ushering me up the stairs, dismissing any of my protestations that I should help her with the washing up.

'Don't be silly Kate. I've had ten days of blissful relaxation. You on the other hand seem not to have slept in this time. Get to bed!'

'Thanks for the dinner,' I mumbled, already half asleep. 'It was delicious.'

The following morning I sat on the tube, clutching a coffee as though my life depended on it. I felt drained and worn out already and the day was only starting. As I sipped the double shot Americano, I decided that I probably did have a caffeine addiction but that as addictions go it was probably the cheapest of the lot.

I got off at Charing Cross station and as I caught myself seriously contemplating buying another coffee, I decided I definitely had a caffeine addiction.

Basil had sent me a text this morning in his usual polite way telling me to go to Charing Cross police station as we had three clients in custody. Two of them were Romanian and had been arrested for theft and the other was an eighteen year old regular client of ours in for robbery.

As I waited in the reception area of the station on a cold metal chair, I pulled my coat tighter around me in the hope that it would provide extra warmth. Despite the deep sleep I had fallen into last night I still felt wiped out and this in turn was making me feel the December chill even more. My conversation with Laura from last night floated into my head. I couldn't believe the difference the holiday had made to her. She looked tanned, calm and her under eye circles had disappeared. Moreover she seemed to have a whole new perspective on life. I was hoping that my four days off at Christmas would have the same affect on me.

'Miss Hunter?' an officer called out, as he poked his head through a partially opened door. Let the fun begin I thought as I stood, bracing myself for the custody suite. The desk was surrounded by various officers, people being checked into custody and the phones were ringing constantly. There was a general sense of chaos prevailing. As I waited in line behind two other solicitors for custody details, a large male who was about to be checked in suddenly kicked off. He went for the petite female officer who was standing closest to him and in the blink of an eye he was being restrained by five custody officers on the floor. He struggled like a fish on the floor before finally realising that his strength was no match for the officers.

Eventually he stood and although he wasn't trying to physically fight the officers any more he didn't hold back on the abuse he was shouting at them. He was forcibly walked to his cell and his voice got louder and the threats more violent as he got closer to his confinement area. As the door was closed to his cell I could hear 'I'll motherfuckin' fuck you up and then I'll fuck up your wife and your children. You're so fucked.'

He continued screaming and shouting for the next ten minutes and either after realising that no one was paying any attention to him or running out of energy, the noise from his cell finally subsided.

'Is he one of yours?' I jokingly asked the solicitors in front of me in the queue.

'He could be,' the older of the two said with a grimace. 'I'm duty for the next two hours so I could get a call about him.'

'What a charmer eh?' the other solicitor added. I recognised his face, probably from around court but I couldn't think of his name.

'Miss Hunter,' the officer for my Romanian clients said, interrupting our banter.

'The interpreter is ready via videolink so if you'd like to get disclosure please follow me.'

As I followed the officer towards a consultation room I could almost guess what he would tell me in disclosure.

As the officer and I settled ourselves in chairs at opposite sides of the table, he played with the remote control to get a live link to the interpreter. Her clear image popped up on the screen and the officer explained to her that he was about to give me disclosure and that she would soon be needed for my consultation with the clients and then for the interview.

'I might as well give you disclosure for both clients now Miss Hunter,' he said sliding four sheets of paper across the desk. 'As you'll see the way the offence was committed in both are very similar.'

I read through the first one for Mr. Balcescu.

'Mr. Balcescu was arrested for theft last night at 19.06 in Hamleys Toy store on Regents Street. He made no reply to caution.

He was seen by store detectives to enter the shop carrying a large shopping bag. He was with another male. They appeared to spend a long time looking at various items in the store. He has been captured on CCTV and seen by the store detectives to place two *board games, a teddy bear and a spinning top into the bag and leave without paying. He was stopped by shop security and searched. Police were called.*

He does not have any previous convictions.'

As I absorbed this information I considered whether I needed any further information from the officer.

'Would you consider a caution?' I asked.

'All options will be considered. As you'll see his friend Mr. Korzha is a different matter altogether because of his previous record.

I read through Mr. Korzha's disclosure which was identical to Mr. Balcescu's except for the last line, which read, '*Mr. Korzha has three previous convictions for theft and was released from prison two weeks ago for serving a sentence for theft.'*

'I guess he's not suitable for a caution then,' I joked.

'I shouldn't think so Miss. Hunter,' he said with a smile.

'Ok shall we start with Mr. Balcescu then?' I asked.

'Certainly. I'll bring him down now.'

As I was waiting for my client to arrive, I used the time to fill out the various forms which needed completing at the station.

As Mr. Balcescu was settling himself, the officer began trying to reengage contact with the interpreter. He appeared to be having a little difficulty this time. After a few moments fiddling around with various switches and pushing random buttons he seemed to have managed to gain contact with her again. Although it seemed more out of luck than through any knowledge of how the system worked. I wondered would he have the same struggle for Mr. Korzha.

The officer left the room and I began the slow process of trying to explain through an interpreter, that my advice was free and that I was completely independent of the police. He haltingly admitted that he had gone into the toy store with his friend, with the foil lined bag to take some items. He said the items were going to be for his children for Christmas as he couldn't afford to buy presents for them.

He kept repeating the words 'I sorry, I sorry,' in English. I felt very sorry for him. The poor man looked as though he hadn't eaten a decent meal in a long time and he had simply been trying to give his children some sense of a normal Christmas. I imagined that everything else in their life was anything but normal. He told me that he had travelled to London from Romania by bus with his wife and two children. He had been hoping to work but it seemed that he was living on the streets with his family. He was apprehensive about what was going to happen at the police station. I tried to reassure him and told him that my advice was free and that he should explain in interview exactly what he had told me. We discussed the possibility that he might get a caution and that in order for this to happen he had to give a full and frank admission during interview. He seemed relieved when he realised that he wouldn't be going straight to prison

When I felt that he completely understood everything that was going to happen, I called the officer back in for interview. When the officer entered the room Mr. Balcescu tensed up one again.

CHAPTER TWENTY SIX

Four hours after I had entered the station, I sat across from Asad Daar, a client I had been representing on and off for the last two years. I hadn't left the small room, except for a toilet break after the interviews with the Romanians had finished. My stomach gave an occasional growl and I had a headache forming.

'I'm tellin' ya Miss I ain't done nothin',' he said heatedly.

If I had a pound for every time I had heard those words I thought wryly to myself.

I took a deep breath. 'Ok Asad. Let's go through this all again,' I said calmly. I needed to keep him relaxed.

'The police have a statement from a pizza delivery man which states that he was attacked by a Somalian looking male with a hammer. He continues that he was struck in the shoulder with this hammer and that the attacker then began demanding that he hand over all his cash and mobile phone. He handed over the cash and said that he didn't have a mobile phone and at this point the attacker pushed him on the floor calling him a Liar. He says the attacker then kicked him several times in the chest area, before walking off.'

'Wasn' me innit,' he said sullenly in response.

'The difficulty you have Assad is that the police found you nearby and you had the same amount of cash on you which was taken from the delivery man. Also they have recovered the hammer and are testing it for fingerprints. The fact that you have a previous conviction for robbery doesn't help much either. I know you're saying you weren't there but if for any reason you think that you might have been, it's best that you go 'no comment' at interview.'

'Ya alright then, but I ain't got no-one who will say I was with 'em to prove I didn' rob someone.'

'Don't worry about that for now Assad, just focus on the interview. I don't want you to put forward a version of events now that you may decide is not actually how it happened at a later point. It's best that you say nothing and see what evidence the police have. Let them prove their case against you. Don't help them do it ok?'

'Ya your right ain't ya Miss. No Comment all the way innit,' he said nodding his head with approval.

'Ok unless you have any questions Asad, I'll call the detectives in and we can get started.'

'Nah, let's just get goin.'

After an hour and a half of listening to the detectives pummel Asad with questions and accusations the interview finally concluded. He had done remarkably well and answered all questions with 'no comment'. This is harder to do than it sounds and Asad looked as shattered as I felt.

As he was put back in his cell, I imagined that he would be charged with robbery and remanded for court until the morning. Before I left the station, I went to the custody desk to see if there had been a decision made with regards to the Romanians. It was considerably quieter now than it had been this morning and the Custody Sergeant even gave me a wide smile before logging into his computer to see if there was a result for me.

'Mr. Balcescu has been cautioned for theft and Mr Korzha has been charged with theft and remanded for court until the morning,' he said cheerfully.

'Thanks, will that be City of Westminster Magistrates?'

'It will indeed love.'

As I left the station, I felt weak with hunger. It was gone four o' clock and I hadn't eaten anything today apart from a slice of toast this morning. I walked quickly to the nearest sandwich shop and sat hungrily devouring a sandwich. I felt calmer after eating and sat sipping my tea, watching the world go by outside.

I sent Basil a quick text telling him the results of today's interviews and that I wouldn't be able to attend Westminster tomorrow to represent Mr. Korzha as I was attending at Camberwell Green Youth Court for Scott Ryan.

I checked the time on my phone. It was almost five o clock. I *should* really head back to the office and try and do some paperwork but it was Christmas week I reasoned with myself. I had just decided to treat myself to a stroll around the shops when I remembered my wheelie bag which was lying at my feet. I really didn't have the energy for lugging that around the crowds. There was nothing for it then. I would just have to go home, I thought cheerily. As I walked towards the tube, the bustling streets and twinkling Christmas decorations lifted my spirits and even being jostled aside as I was trying to get on a train didn't dampen them.

I was almost humming Christmas carols by the time I turned to walk up our drive. I froze half way up. Lying in the exact same position as before was a single red rose with a card attached to it. Was someone watching me right now?

I contemplated leaving the rose where it was but I scooped it up and threw myself against the door as I twisted the key. Once inside I bolted all the locks and switched on the light. My legs felt shaky so I sat down on the bottom step of the stairs. With trembling hands I separated the card from the cellophane. It was exactly the same as the others. However the inscription was different. It read,

'Kate they are trying to keep us apart but I know that you are my friend and want to support me. I will fix this. Nothing will keep me from spending time with you.'

I was now certain that it was Shane. He must have found out that I'd no longer be dealing with his case.

Suddenly the doorbell sounded loudly and someone was knocking on the door. My heart began pounding. Had he taken things a step further and dared to arrive at my door?

'Kate, Kate! Are you in there? Let me in!' a female voice shouted loudly.

It was Laura. My heart slowed its frantic beating. As I opened the door she almost hit me in the face as she was just about to knock on the door again.

'What's going on? Why's the door locked?' she asked sounding slightly irritated. It was only then that I remembered her saying last night that she would be leaving work early today because she had a Christmas party to get ready for.

A look of understanding washed over her face as she eyed the rose which lay at her feet. I had bought her up to speed last night and she couldn't believe how long I had taken to tell Basil that I wasn't dealing with Shane anymore. She knew all about Shane's previous 'love letters' to me. We used to be in hysterics as I recounted what they said. However as Laura had put it last night, I didn't exactly deal with the most 'savoury of individuals and I didn't know what they were capable of'. I had always thought of Shane as harmless but the reality was that he was capable of ferocious violence. His previous convictions for Grievous Bodily Harm confirmed this. With hindsight I should probably have offloaded him to Nick a long time ago.

'Hey, you need to start getting ready for tonight!' I

said trying to lighten the mood. I knew Laura was extremely excited about this party as 'Hot guy' was going to be there.

'Are you sure Kate? I think maybe I should stay with you tonight.'

'Don't be silly. Go to the party. I want a full progress report on 'Hot Guy' tomorrow morning,' I said with a jollity I didn't really feel. I knew Laura wouldn't go if she felt that I was worried about being on my own.

'Are you sure?' she repeated.

'Honestly Laura, I'll be totally fine.' I must have sounded very reassuring because Laura bounded up the stairs and within moments I could hear the water of the shower running.

A little later as I was pondering what to have for dinner, Laura whirled into the room for a final inspection before she jumped into her taxi.

'Wow you look amazing!' I said sincerely. Her glowing tan, black dress and blonde curls were a great combination.

'Thanks Kate,' she said hugging me. 'Seriously if you want me to come back at any time at all just ring me ok?'

'Thanks Laura. Enjoy your night.'

That night I slept restlessly. I spent most of it tossing and turning as various thoughts floated in and out of my mind. What was Shane thinking? Did he honestly believe that we were close friends? His words from after the bail hearing kept coming back to me. 'A girl I like.' Was that me?

CHAPTER TWENTY SEVEN

Then next morning on the bus to Camberwell Green Magistrates Court, I sent Nick a text.

Another rose on my doorstep last night. I'm more convinced than ever that it's Shane. By any chance do you know if he contacted the office looking for me yesterday. I wasn't in-Charing Cross all day

After a few minutes of flicking through the Metro, Nick text back.

No way! Kate this is getting serious. We need to talk properly about what to do. Yes he called in yesterday afternoon to see you and was none too pleased when he found out that I would be dealing with him in the future. Was shouting so loudly Basil came into the office.

I groaned. No doubt Basil was furious that a regular client was unhappy. I hadn't explained exactly why I didn't want to deal with Shane anymore in my email to him. I had simply said that there was a clash of personalities which couldn't be resolved and that Nick had offered to take him on as a client. Basil had been extremely reluctant to agree the transfer so my guess was I was definitely not in his good books today.

Thanks for dealing with him for me. I bet Basil's veins were about to pop! Good luck today at court. Chat later

As I walked from the bus stop to the Courthouse, my thoughts moved from Shane to Scott Ryan whose case was listed in the Youth court. He had been charged with robbery and GBH and today's hearing would decide whether his case would proceed at the youth court or whether the court would send his case to the Crown Court for trial.

Walking through the defunct security scanner, I

wondered why they were so lax with security at this particular youth court. It seemed strange, especially as there were so many gangs operating around this area. I suppose the silver lining was that I didn't get my handbag rifled through.

As I hauled my wheelie up the stairs, I was jostled by someone, obviously eager to get to the top. He grunted an apology and I realised I recognised his face.

'Andrew, hi, I didn't realise you were in court today.' I had represented him at the police station a couple of weeks ago and knew he wasn't in court for that matter. I wondered if he was using another firm?

'I'm not Miss,' he said in his sullen way. It didn't look like he was going to expand on why he was here, but my guess one of his friends was listed to appear before the court for something. He continued up the stairs ahead of me and his trousers were so low-slung I could see that he was wearing blue and white stripped boxer shorts. Well at least I hadn't lost a client I thought to myself.

Upstairs, I saw Scott sitting meekly on a blue metal chair. His terrified look made him stand out as a first-timer in court. I walked over and a wave of relief seemed to wash over his face.

'Morning Scott. How are you doing?'

'I'm ok,' he said quietly.

'Right Scott, I said sitting down beside him. Let me explain what's going to happen today in court ok? Is your father with you?' I asked looking around the busy waiting area.

He shook his head. Youths under seventeen were supposed to have an adult with them at court and I knew that the judge would ask me to explain why Scott hadn't brought a parent along with him.

My guess was that his father simply couldn't be bothered to attend or that he was down at the pub, but I needed some sort of explanation from Scott.

'Any particular reason why he couldn't come with you?' I asked gently.

'I don't know. I haven't seen him in a couple of days.'

It was then that I noticed the bruising on his face.

'Scott, what happened to your face?'

'Nothin', just leave it ok?' he said quietly.

I decided not to press the issue. I did wonder silently however whether Mr. Ryan had done this to Scott.

Just then, out of the corner of my eye I saw the Prosecutor enter Courtroom 5 where Scott's case was listed.

'Scott, the lady that just went into that Courtroom over there is the Prosecutor who will be dealing with your case. I'm going to have a chat with her now and get your papers. Then I'll come back and we'll discuss your plea and fill out some legal aid forms. Okay?'

Scott silently nodded his head.

Inside the courtroom three advocates had beaten me to it and formed a queue in front of the Prosecutors bench. As I stood waiting, I could feel my phone vibrate in my pocket. It was from Nick.

You should have seen the Romanians face when I told him about the hardline that City of Westminster were taking when sentencing for theft. Don't think he expected to be in prison for Crimbo!

I smiled. City of Westminster Magistrates Court was now giving custodial sentences of up to 18 weeks to all first time offenders. This would be reduced to 12 weeks if clients pleaded guilty at the earliest opportunity. I wondered what Mr. Korzha would get, as he had previous for theft.

Eventually the Prosecutor was ready to deal with me.

'Good morning,' I greeted her. 'I'm looking for

papers for Scott Ryan please.'

'Ah yes, little Mr. Ryan, with no previous convictions,' she said sounding cranky. I took this to mean that she had just recently read his file. 'So what are the Crown saying about venue for the case?' I asked. As these were very serious charges, the Prosecution could argue for the case to be sent to the Crown Court.

'Suitable for the Youth Court,' she said as she handed me the relevant papers. I felt my shoulders relax a little. I hadn't been looking forward to having a legal argument about which court this case should be heard in. Scott would find it a lot less daunting having his case heard here rather than at the Crown court.

Before heading back to Scott, I decided to dump my coat and bag in the tiny advocate's room. I also slipped on my heels and stuffed my flats into my bag.

Once I was back sitting beside Scott, I could feel the tension radiating from his body. I would have loved to have been able to have a consultation in a private room but unfortunately, this courthouse, like so many more around London was poor on such resources.

As I began to fill out the legal aid form with Scott, I noticed that his eyes were fixed on something across the hallway. When I looked across, I saw Andrew, leaning against the wall with his arms folded across his chest. He was with two other boys of about sixteen that I didn't recognise. All three of them were staring directly at Scott, who looked terrified.

'Do you know those boys Scott?' I asked before returning to filling out the form.

Scott seemed unable to tear his eyes away from the boys.

'Scott,' I said quite loudly, trying to break the trancelike state he was in.

As he looked sideways at me, I could see a look of

fear in his eyes.

'Do you know those boys Scott?' I repeated gently.

When he didn't answer after a few moments, I decided to drop it. I had more important things to think about than Scott's social connections.

'Scott do you remember what you said in your interview about this matter? You said the only reason you did it was because you felt you had no other choice if you wanted to join the gang which would offer you protection. Do you remember?'

Scott seemed terribly distracted.

'Are you still saying the same thing?'

Scott didn't answer. This was like pulling teeth.

'Scott you need to help me out here. I can only advise you on how you should plead. But only you can decide what you actually want to do.' Dealing with youths was tricky, particularly if they arrived without a parent.

Suddenly Scott seemed to burst into life. 'Guilty. I'm pleading guilty,' he blurted out.

'Ok, well Scott, from what we discussed at your police station interview, I understood that you wanted to plead not guilty on the basis that you were acting under duress.' I knew that this would be difficult to prove at trial, but it may be possible to get it through but it would probably very much depend on what judge we would get.

'Are you sure that you want to plead guilty today? If you do, obviously you will credit for your early guilty plea, which means that you would get a lower sentence than if you were convicted after trial. There is the option of pleading guilty 'on a certain basis' though Scott which I think might be worth considering.' I saw the look of confusion in his eyes so went on to explain what this meant.

'What this means is that you would be pleading

guilty. However we would write out the basis on which you were pleading guilty. In your case this would allow us to explain to the court why you acted like you did. The tricky part though is that we would have to get the prosecutor to agree to accept this basis of plea which can be quite difficult to do. What do you think? Do you want to give it a shot?'

'No,' he said resolutely. 'I'm pleading guilty. Just the normal pleading guilty. Not what you just explained to me.'

He seemed a bit more relaxed now that he had made that decision.

'What's going to happen to me? Am I going to prison today?'

'No Scott. You won't be going to prison today. Generally first time youth offenders will be given a referral order as a sentence. What this means is that you will have to engage with the youth offending team for whatever period the court thinks is appropriate. In your case, because the offences are very serious, I think that the Court will adjourn the matter so as the Youth Offending Team can prepare a report on you. They will generally suggest a sentence that the court usually follows.'

'Will I be going to prison then?' he interrupted.

'No Scott,' I said patiently. 'If you were an adult, you would more than likely get a custodial sentence for these offences. However as you are a youth I think the Youth Offending Team might suggest either a Referral Order or a Youth Rehabilitation Order. Do you know what that means?'

Scott shook his head.

'The YOT would ask you a lot of questions about your life and identify what areas they felt that you needed extra support or help with. They would then suggest a programme which would address those needs.

Also there is the possibility that a curfew could be put in place as a form of punishment.'

It seemed like my explanation had fallen on deaf ears as Scott looked as though he was lost in a trance again. He was once again staring across the room, in the direction of Andrew who was staring right back at him.

Suddenly I knew exactly what was going on. I knew Andrew was in a gang and I suspected that it was the same one that Scott wanted to join. It was more than likely that Andrew and his two friends had been sent here to ensure that Scott wouldn't do anything stupid like plead not guilty and go to trial on this.

'Scott come with me,' I said standing.

Obediently, he stood and trailed after me. His newness to the court system was so blatant. Most youths wouldn't unquestionably follow me.

There was no room in the courthouse where we could have a private conversation. I led him into the cramped Advocates room which thankfully was empty. I turned to face him. His face was crumpled into a look of puzzlement.

'Scott, are you pleading guilty because someone has told you to?'

He remained silent.

'Scott?'

Again silence.

'Scott, would you be afraid for your safety if you pleaded not guilty?'

'I don't want to talk about it,' he said quietly.

'Because if you are Scott, and you tell me, I can try and help you.'

'I want to plead guilty,' he said without looking me in the eye.

I stared back at him, weighing up my options. I didn't have any doubt now that Scott was pleading guilty because he wanted to join the gang. What could I do? He wasn't the first youth who wanted to join a gang, no matter what it took, and he certainly wouldn't be the last. I decided to have one last attempt at making him open up.

'Scott are you sure?' I said gently. 'There are ways that you can be made feel safe.'

He shook his head and I could see from the look in his eyes that his mind was made up. Like so many other kids, he thought that the only way to survive in his world was to join a gang. It probably wouldn't be long before Scott was well and truly involved in their world and it was more than likely that I would be seeing him around police stations and courts a lot in the future.

I sighed. 'Okay Scott, it's up to you. I'll tell the list-caller that we're ready and hopefully we won't have too long a wait until we're called on.'

Much later as I was leaving court, I saw a group of four black youths with hoods up, huddled together smoking. It was dark but as I walked by, I could make out that it was Andrew, his two mates and Scott. Andrew gave me an almost imperceptible nod. Scott had obviously passed the test. He had bought into gang life which might make him feel safe in the short term but I was certain that in the long term Scott had just sold his freedom and that a life of crime lay ahead of him. Initially I had thought that the marks on his face had been caused by his father. Now I suspected that someone in the gang had caused them.

The District Judge had created a big fuss about Scott's parents not being present at court and had ordered that when Scott would be sentenced in three weeks time that one or both of them were to attend. I doubted that either of them would come to court. As I had expected the Judge had ordered that the Youth

Offending Team should prepare a report before Scott would be sentenced.

It was four o' clock, cold and windy and the last thing I wanted to do was go back to the office. However I knew that Nick would be there. He had sworn that he was going to make a dent in his paperwork pile before Christmas. I really wanted to talk to him about the roses and Shane Reid, so I reluctantly trudged towards the bus stop lost in thought about Scott Ryan and the way his life was likely to go from now on. I suspected I would be seeing a lot more of him in the future.

CHAPTER TWENTY EIGHT

Back at the 'base', as Nick liked to call it, I hurriedly walked past Basil's office. I could hear him roaring down the phone at some poor unfortunate. Not for the first time I wondered what had happened in his life to make him so *angry.*

'She has returned,' Nick exclaimed when I walked into our office. From the crossword he held in his hands, I could tell he was making great progress with his paperwork!

'I know, I know,' he said guiltily, holding up the crossword. 'It's just far more entertaining than *that,*' he said nodding in the direction of his paperwork.

'Hey, who am I to judge?' I said collapsing into my chair, as I eyed the large bundle of paperwork that awaited my attention.

'How amazing would it be to have a secretary?' I thought out loud.

'No point in dreaming Kate. With all these legal aid cuts we're lucky to have jobs ourselves,' Nick replied.

Not wanting to get into a 'state of legal aid' chat I offered to make tea.

'Yes please,' Nick said eagerly. I could see that he wanted any distraction to avoid having to do some work.

A little while later it almost felt cosy, as we sat sipping our tea. Deciding I couldn't avoid the issue anymore I asked about Shane.

Nick took a sip from his mug before answering. 'There's not really a lot to say. He came in looking to speak to you. When the receptionist directed him to me he started shouting about how people were conspiring to keep him from seeing you. It was all quite dramatic

197

really.'

'Did you actually have a meeting with him?'

'There was no chance of that. He was really irate and didn't even sit down.'

'Why did he want to see me?'

'The only coherent thing he said, was that he needed to discuss bail conditions with you. The rest was a rant about how we were all keeping him from seeing you.'

'How does Basil feature in all of this?'

'Ooh Kate you should have seen him!' Nick said almost gleefully. 'He was literally purple and I thought the veins in his neck were going to pop.'

'Oh dear,' I sighed. 'I didn't really explain in the email I sent to him about why I wanted to hand him over as a client. I imagine Basil thinks I'm just being difficult.'

'Probably,' Nick agreed.

'Hopefully I'll be able to avoid him until after Christmas and maybe he'll have cooled off a little by then,' I said. Although I knew that Basil had a great ability to hold a grudge, so I wasn't going to get my hopes up.

'Do you think that Shane went straight from here to your house in Clapham and dropped off the rose?' Nick asked, his eyebrows raised.

'Sometimes I feel like I'm being completely paranoid about it all,' I said wearily. 'But I just can't think of any other explanation for it. I was hoping that when you took over his case I wouldn't receive any more roses, so last night's one really freaked me out. I just don't know what to do..' I trailed off.

Eventually I spoke, 'I know that he's capable of being violent. His previous convictions show that. But he has never been anything but docile with me so maybe I'm overreacting?'

'I don't think so Kate. It almost seems like he's

developed an obsession with you. We don't have any proof though which we could take to the police, do we?'

'No and as I said with his bail conditions he's not even supposed to be in Clapham. But unless he's seen there and arrested for breach of bail I don't know what else I can do. I think I'll just wait until after Christmas and see if anything else happens. Maybe that's the end of it now?' I said hopefully.

Nick didn't say anything but looked at me sceptically.

'So what are your Christmas plans?' I asked Nick, eager to get off the topic of Shane Reid. As Nick started talking about how he and his girlfriend Milly were trying to spend their time equally with both families I started to get a little excited about Christmas. I had been so busy with work that I hadn't really let myself get into the festive spirit. I was on call tonight and working tomorrow but the party with Alex at his parents house would begin my four day break very nicely.

Nick eventually decided that he should try and tackle some of the paperwork on his desk and I made a half hearted attempt to do the same. At about seven o' clock he decided to call it a day and left the office humming Christmas tunes. I sat trying to decide whether I should hang around a little longer or head home. I was on duty for Central London Police stations until mid-night and it would be just my luck to head back to Clapham and then have to come back in.

Just as I decided to go home and was wrapping myself up in my coat a call from the Defence Solicitors Call Centre came through.

'Good Evening, Kate speaking.'

'Hello this is the Defence Solicitors Call Centre,' a northern accent said, 'we have a duty case at

Bishopsgate Police Station. Are you available to take the details?'

'Yes,' I said fumbling to get a pen from the top drawer of my desk.

'Can I take your pin number first please?'

'Sure, it's 12987.'

'Thank you. It's a male adult called Adelmo Silva. He's Chilean and will require a Spanish interpreter. Arrested at 10.00 this morning for theft from person and is at Charing Cross Police Station. Will you require any other details?'

As I waited for the lady to give me the reference number I wondered if I would have time to get some dinner before I had to go to the station.

After hanging up, I phoned up the station to get the details of the case and was told that the interpreter and Officers would be ready for interview in an hour and a half.

Mr. Silva was put on the phone to me but after a few minutes of him stuttering in broken English, 'I not understand,' I gave up on the farcical conversation and decided that I would talk to him properly at the station via the interpreter.

CHAPTER TWENTY NINE

About two hours later I sat opposite Mr. Silva, having a consultation with him through the interpreter who appeared in the room with us on a videolink screen. Mr. Silva had been released from prison this morning and just as he was walking out the gates, chuffed to be leaving, he was arrested for a theft he had committed prior to going inside. You really couldn't make this stuff up sometimes! The poor guy was bought straight back into custody.

He had arrived in London about five months ago and had spent most of his stay in prison. At this point he was telling me that he just wanted to go home. Unfortunately for him, my guess was that he would be spending another few months inside.

The police were alleging that he had walked into a bar near Bank with a friend and stolen a handbag with the contents valued at £700. I had seen CCTV footage from the bar and having sat across from Mr. Silva for the last few minutes it was clear that it was him I had seen on the footage.

Despite saying that he understood that I was on his side, he was being very coy about whether or not he had been in the bar that evening. However, there was no denying the fact that he was captured on CCTV. His only concern now seemed to be how long he was going to get sent away for and if I would be at court for him in the morning. After assuring him that I would be, I advised him that he should answer questions with 'no comment' in order to protect himself from self-incrimination. Even though both he and I knew that he was going to be charged with the theft anyway.

I had to hand it to Mr. Silva, the interviewing officer was doing his best to make him talk but he answered all his questions with a resolute 'no comment'. As he was being escorted back to his cell after the interview, my phone rang. It was the Defence Solicitors Call Centre. When this happened a part of me was always happy that I was getting extra work but at 9pm I also just wanted to go home.

It was for another male who had been arrested for theft. Sighing I walked towards the custody desk to find out about this Alexander Thorpe-Warrington. It was certainly rare to get such an English sounding name and from the double barrel surname, I was assuming that he wasn't like my average client. The English legal system provided free and independent legal advice for everyone who was arrested and requested a solicitor at the police station. This happened despite a person's means, so even if Mr. Thorpe Warrington was one of the wealthiest men in London he was still entitled to free legal advice.

When the Custody Sergeant had finished joking with another officer about last night's soccer match, he turned his attention to me.

'Alright luv?'

'I just picked up a call for a Mr. Thorpe Warrington. Do you know any details about the case or if there has been an officer appointed to it yet?'

'Just give me a moment luv,' he said while tapping away at his keyboard. 'Bloody cutbacks mean that these relics which they call computers aren't going to be replaced. Soon we'll be back to the paper and pen. Just waiting for his details to load,' he said tapping his fingers on his desk impatiently.

As I was waiting, I checked my messages. My heart soared when I saw one from Alex.

Can't wait for tomorrow night. Don't work too hard tonight.X

'That from the boyfriend luv?' the custody officer asked with a grin on his face. 'Must be a new one if a text can make you light up like that.'

Was Alex my boyfriend? No, definitely not, I decided, shaking my head. We had only been on a few dates. Although I think I wanted him to be.

'Finally,' the officer said wearily, handing me the custody record for Mr. Thorpe Warrington and breaking my reverie.

'It says here on the system that the OIC is ready for interview.'

I breathed a sigh of relief. I might actually get some sleep tonight.

'Would you like me to call him for you luv?'

'Yes please, that would be great. I'll wait in the consultation room.'

As I sat there waiting for the OIC to arrive, I flicked idly through the Law Gazette, which I had found in a crumpled mess at the bottom of my bag. It made for depressing reading. The headline on the cover couldn't be ignored:

'Best Value Tendering to become a Reality'.'

As long as I had been qualified the Government had been threatening to introduce this. They wanted each firm in the country to tender the lowest price which they could do work for. The most cost effective firms would then be granted contracts to practice defence law. Before my mood could sink any further the OIC burst into the room with a smile, followed by her assisting officer.

'Miss Hunter?'

'Yes,' I couldn't help but smile back at her. Her smile was infectious and made me forget about the Law Gazette which I stuffed back into my bag.

'Are you dealing with Mr. Thorpe-Warrington?'

'Yes, that's right. I've got the custody record from

the officer and am ready for disclosure.'

'Is verbal disclosure okay?'

'Sure,' I said picking up my pen.

'Basically, he went into a Boots store today and after browsing a shelf of moisturisers he put one jar into his pocket. My colleague and I saw him do this. We were operating as plain clothes officers today. This is also captured on CCTV. He then exits the store without paying for it.'

She paused to allow me to scribble down everything that she had said. When I raised my head she continued.

'We then follow him and he walks into another Boots store. He goes straight to the pharmacy counter and asks for a refund for the moisturiser. He is given a credit note, which he immediately uses to buy a box of codeine tablets and a chapstick. He then leaves the store and is arrested by myself.'

'Did he make any significant comments on arrest?' I questioned.

'No, none at all.'

'Any previous convictions?'

'Nothing. He's not the usual shoplifter we have in here,' she added with a smile. 'Obviously it depends on what he says at interview but this matter is definitely suitable for a caution. In fact he may be eligible for a Penalty notice.'

'Ok, can I have a consultation with him in here?'

'We'll bring him down to you straight away Miss Hunter.'

About an hour later, I left the station, thrilled to be going home. I really wanted to get a good night's sleep before Alex's party tomorrow. Fingers crossed I wouldn't get anymore calls before my duty slot ended. As I walked down the steps of Charing Cross tube station, I thought about Mr. Thorpe-Warrington. He was probably the most well spoken client I had encountered so far. It turned out that he had a codeine addiction and was on a very limited allowance from his father. He had paid rent today and was struggling for money to buy the 40 tablets of codeine he was taking daily. I think the few hours in a police cell had terrified him and his relief on receiving a Penalty notice, which was effectively a fine, had been written all over his face. He had thanked me profusely and had just stopped short of hugging me.

On the tube journey my mind wandered to Alex. Even thinking about him made me smile. I had first met him at one of Nick's house parties about two years ago. He had had the same effect on me then and my heart had dropped when I had seen him wrap his arms around his girlfriend at the time. I had been secretly thrilled when I had heard that they had broken up. Nick had started instructing him on more and more work so I began seeing a lot more of him around, much to my delight. I had never expected that he might feel the same about me. Just as I was imagining running my hands through his dark hair the train pulled into Clapham Common tube station.

As I exited the station, I stuffed my hands in my coat pockets and walked briskly home, stopping only in Sainsbury's to get some chocolate. It felt like it had been one of those days. I was looking forward to curling up on the couch with some tea, chocolate and rubbish TV.

'Goddam it,' I muttered to myself as I walked up our drive. A single rose lay on the doorstep, in the exact position as the others had been. This time I felt more annoyed than fearful. Stalking up towards the door, I stooped and picked up the rose, ignoring the card which fluttered to the ground. I slipped the key in the lock and hurled myself at the door and once again, fell into the hallway. Switching on the light, I went directly to the kitchen and dumped the rose in the bin. I felt strangely triumphant. It was as if by not getting scared of the rose and white card, I had taken the power from whoever was leaving them.

Not giving the rose a second thought I changed out of my suit, pulling on leggings and a big cosy jumper. Once I was settled on the couch with the remote, a steaming mug of tea and my family sized bar of chocolate I finally relaxed. After about an hour, I felt myself falling asleep, so hauled myself off the couch and climbed the stairs to my bedroom. Just as I was about to turn off my bedside lamp, I heard the front door open and close. It felt like my heart skipped a beat. Laura had gone home for Christmas this afternoon and no-one other than our landlord had a key for the house. What could I do? I heard footsteps on the stairs.

I grabbed my phone from the bedside locker and had frantically dialled
999, when I heard a familiar voice. Moments later Laura's blonde head appeared through the partially opened door.

'Jesus Laura. I almost called the police. I thought you were...' I broke off.

'Happy Christmas,' Laura slurred drunkenly, throwing herself at me in a clumsy embrace. She started humming Jingle Bells tunelessly.

'I thought you were heading home today for Christmas?' I asked as she disentangled herself from me.

'Was supposed to,' she slurred, standing up unsteadily. 'I kind of got drawn into impromptu office drinks. My mother is not going to be happy.' With that she wandered out of the room and moments later I could hear her clunking around noisily in the kitchen. I snuggled up under the duvet again, trying to calm my racing mind. When I had heard the noises, I thought there was an intruder in the house. Not only that but I had assumed that it was whoever was leaving the roses and that I had pissed them off by not taking the card. If I was completely honest with myself I had believed that it was Shane Reid. After much tossing and turning I eventually fell into a restless sleep.

CHAPTER THIRTY

The following morning, as I sat in the cells of Westminster Magistrates Court, speaking with Mr. Silva through an interpreter, I felt far more rational than I had last night. I had convinced myself that I had completely overreacted and now my thoughts were on tonight and the party at Alex's parents. I was excited as I hadn't seen him in a few days but also nervous. Was this an actual 'meet the parents' party or was I just going as Alex's date?

'Sorry?'I said jolting back to reality.

I looked from the interpreter to Mr. Silva for some indication as to what had been said.

The interpreter spoke. 'He wants to know if there is any way of convincing the judge that he would complete a Community Order?' She almost said this with a smile. From our consultation she was well aware of Mr. Silva's history in this country. Even if he didn't have any previous convictions, Westminster Magistrates Court tough new sentencing policy would mean that he would get a minimum twelve week custodial sentence even if he was a first time offender.

I shook my head. 'Unfortunately Mr. Silva, because of your previous convictions and the court you are appearing in today, you will definitely be going back to prison to serve a sentence.' I stopped and waited for the interpreter to translate this.

I could see from the unsurprised and almost indifferent expression on his face that he had been expecting this. Sometimes people in his situation clung to some hope of a miracle. The reality was that the courts had sentencing guidelines to follow and from whatever angle you looked at it Mr. Silva was going to be going back to prison.

'Ok Mr. Silva, unless you have any other questions I'll see you upstairs.'

After this had been interpreted, he shook his head. I suspected that he was regretting coming to the UK.

As I signed out of the cells, I saw four officers restraining a thin, sweaty male on the floor. Despite being outnumbered he wasn't giving up without a struggle. Some of the others in custody, who were in cells close by, started banging their doors in support. Spending time in police and court cells could be mind-numbingly boring for many so any sort of distraction was welcomed. As I waited for a door release to leave the cells, I saw the male stop struggling. Either he had used up all his energy or he had realised that he was greatly outnumbered. His face took on a look of resignation.

As I climbed the stairs, which seemed to be my only exercise at the moment, I spied Nicks back. I would recognise that hair anywhere.

'Hey! What are you doing lurking on the stairs?' I said.

He turned, his face breaking into a smile when he saw me.

'Kate! I don't suppose you can go for a quick coffee? Apparently someone cancelled my Urdu interpreter so I can't get one here now before 3pm. I have a lot of time to kill,' he said checking his watch. I knew it was only 10.30am.

'I hate it when that happens. You could go back to the office,' I joked. I knew the office was the last place Nick would go back to. He pulled a face, as if to confirm he would rather be anywhere than our little room in Chancery Lane.

'I should really try and get on with my Chilean. I'm kind of hoping to finish a bit early today.'

'Does Basil know about your cavalier attitude to

timekeeping Miss Hunter?' he asked with a smirk.

'I'm sure Basil would self-combust if he knew I was thinking of skiving off. Let me check with the list-caller to see how soon I can get on. If it's going to be ages then you're in luck. I'll see you in the Advocates room?'

'Yes, I suppose it's better than me lurking on the stairs like this.'

I entered courtroom four and bowed to the Magistrates. They were in the middle of sentencing a middle-aged man for what sounded like domestic assault. I crouched down beside the list-caller.

'Morning. I'm representing Mr. Silva. We're ready to go. How long do you think until our case can be called on?' I whispered.

'You're in luck. At the moment I don't have any other cases ready so you can get on after this sentencing.'

Excellent, I thought. Hopefully I'll be able to get this case done and then go for coffee with Nick. I sat behind the Defence advocate whose case was being heard and sent Nick a quick text.

Just about to be called on. Shouldn't be long. He's definitely getting custody. See you in advocate's room then for coffee ☺

Just then, the man who was being sentenced broke down crying, big heaving sobs.

'I didn't mean to do it,' he sniffled. 'I won't do it again. Please?' he said looking imploringly at the Magistrates, who were steadfastly looking at their notebooks, which lay on the bench in front of them.

As the Gaolers tried to get him to walk through the door which lead back down to the cells, he began struggling. His eyes had a look of wild terror in them. All he was doing was putting off the inevitable but he seemed to think that if he held fast the Magistrates would have a change of heart and not send him into custody. After a few more minutes of heaving sobs about how he was going to miss Christmas with his children, he eventually seemed to give in and followed the Gaolers through the door. His sobbing could still be heard through the thick door as he was lead back downstairs.

The minute he was gone the list-caller was on her feet, eager to start crossing names off her long list.

'The next matter is Mr. Silva, in custody, represented by Miss Hunter.'

'Good morning your worships,' I said standing.

'Any indication of a plea?' the court clerk asked.

'Guilty,' I replied, before sitting down.

Mr. Silva was bought through the same door that the previous male had disappeared through. The interpreter was sworn in and Mr. Silva entered a guilty plea. After the prosecutor had read the facts I mitigated on his behalf. In his circumstances there wasn't a lot that could be said to improve his situation. The fact that he had only been in England for a few months and had spent the majority of this time in custody spoke volumes. When I had finished the Magistrates took all of about thirty seconds to decide that Mr. Silva was going to receive a custodial sentence. He was given credit for his early guilty plea which meant that he received a 12 weeks sentence. He would probably be out after 6 weeks.

As I left the courtroom, I sent Nick a quick text.

Just popping down to the cells for a post-court consultation. See you at the front door in twenty?

A reply pinged back quickly.

You're a life-saver!

CHAPTER THIRTY ONE

That evening as I was getting ready to go to Alex's, Nicks words rang in my ears. He had issued yet another warning about taking care of myself. I almost regretted telling him about the rose that had been left last night. Now he seemed to think I should go to the police. Part of me felt that he was right but also part of me felt that I was really only speculating that it was Shane who was leaving the flowers. What if I went to the police on what could be just my overactive imagination and Shane was arrested for breaching his bail conditions. With his record he would definitely be remanded. Could I do that to him without knowing for certain that it was him?

I decided to pour myself a drink in an attempt to cheer myself up and get in the mood for Alex's party. After rummaging around in the kitchen cupboards for a while, I found a half full bottle of gin. After pouring myself a generous measure and adding the tonic and ice, I was feeling a little more in the mood for a party. As thoughts of Shane and the roses floated out of my mind, I began wondering about the party tonight. It would be interesting to see Alex in the home where he grew up. I wondered what his parents would be like?

About an hour later, I was in remarkably better spirits. This may have been due to the fact that I'd almost finished the bottle of the gin and as I'd run out of tonic, the last one had been a shot which had hit me straight away. Originally Alex had said he would pick me up but I didn't want him disappearing on his parents so I'd assured him I would get a cab. I justified the extravagance because I didn't want to ruin the Christian Louboutins Laura had loaned me for the night. I probably wouldn't have made it up and down the tube steps in them anyway.

As I was checking that everything I needed was in my tiny clutch, I had a text to say that the taxi was outside waiting for me. I checked myself one last time in the mirror. I had been a little stressed about what to wear to meet his parents and had settled on a black dress. It could be seen as boring but I didn't want to wear anything too daring and frighten his mother. Paired with the Louboutins, I hoped that the look was elegant and classy. I sprayed on a little more perfume and walked slowly down the stairs, gripping the banister as I went. These shoes really didn't allow any fast movements. Now I understood why people called them 'taxi shoes'!

About twenty minutes later, the taxi turned off Gloucester Road in Kensington and drove slowly along a quiet street lined with beautiful old buildings. I could see Christmas lights twinkling within the homes.

'This alright luv?' the taxi man asked, looking at me in his rear-view mirror.

'Yes, perfect thank you,' I said handing him the exact fare.

As I stepped out of the car, I stared in wonder at the house in front of me. I had known Alex came from a wealthy family but I hadn't expected a house of this size, in one of the most expensive areas of London.

As I walked up the drive I could hear music and laughter. I toyed with the idea of texting Alex to tell him I had arrived but I decided to be brave and ring the doorbell as every other guest had done. I had purposely arrived a bit late so his parents would be busy entertaining their guests and I wouldn't be the main focus of their attention.

After ringing the doorbell, I waited anxiously. I was almost expecting a butler to open the door. Instead it was flung open by someone who looked like a slightly younger version of Alex. I smiled at his enthusiasm.

'You must be Kate,' he said in greeting.

I tried to hide my surprise but obviously didn't do a very good job because the Alex lookalike went on to explain.

'All of my parent's guests are almost at retirement age. You're the only lady who is young enough or good looking enough to be Alex's girlfriend.'

Girlfriend! Is that what Alex was calling me.

Once again my face must have betrayed me as he hurriedly went on to introduce himself, anxious to get off the topic of my relationship status.

'I'm Max,' he said ushering me into the hallway, which was probably the size of our entire ground floor in Clapham.

'Can I take your coat?'

'Yes. Please,' I said shrugging it off and handing it to him. Out of nowhere a uniformed waitress appeared with a tray of champagne glasses. I gratefully took the glass Max handed to me.

'Let me give you the guided tour,' Max smiled. Alex has probably been accosted by some cougar type. He's very popular with the older ladies! They find him utterly charming.'

'Is that a touch of jealousy I sense?' I said teasingly. I was beginning to relax. I wasn't sure whether it was the bubbles or Max putting me at ease but I didn't feel as terrified as I had a few minutes ago. Max guided me into what I presumed was the sitting room. In the corner, there was a pianist playing festive songs and people were milling around, stopping to chat or take a drink from the ever present waitress's tray. Even Scrooge would have been tempted to get into the festive spirit in this atmosphere.

As we walked through the room, Max nodded and smiled at various people.

'I have no idea who most of these people are,' he said quietly as we walked into a large conservatory. Just when I was wondering when I would get to see Alex, I spotted him across the room smiling and nodding at something a distinguished looking man was saying to him. Just then he moved his head in our direction, catching me admiring him. He winked and moments later he excused himself and began moving through the crowd towards us. My heart began beating faster and I was willing myself to stay calm. He had a way of completely disarming me.

'Kate, I see you've met Max,' he said brushing his lips against mine. I almost closed my eyes, forgetting that Max was standing right beside me.

'I'm afraid I can't stay and chat,' Max said, looking a little disappointed. 'I better get back to my door duties. It was lovely finally meeting you Kate,' he said turning towards me. Hopefully we'll get to talk later.' With that he was gone. Alex and I were alone together.

'I was beginning to worry you wouldn't come,' Alex said.

'Taxi trouble,' I said in an off-hand way.

'I'm so glad you could come,' Alex said softly. ' I was worried that it might seem too soon to invite you to a party at my parents house but I really enjoy spending time with you Kate and I wanted you to meet them.'

I almost melted. He wasn't calling me his girlfriend but he liked me enough to be introducing me to his parents. I felt like I was floating. Alex handed me another glass of champagne from the ubiquitous waitress. I really should slow down on the alcohol I thought. I didn't want to throw up on his parents. I took a sip. It just tasted so good.

'Did Max give you the full tour?' he asked.

'Well, he showed me the room in there,' I said indicating with my hand, 'and this beautiful room.'

'Come on,' he said putting his hand around my waist. It felt so natural for him to guide me like this. Usually if a guy had acted like this with me I would have run a mile by now, but for some reason with Alex it felt right. As he showed me around the house I marvelled at how huge it was. At one point, as we walked by a hall table upstairs, I stopped to look at childhood photos of him. I couldn't help but laugh at Alex as a four year old. He had blonde curly hair, a beaming smile and was covered in chocolate.

'I had a sweet tooth, even back then,' he joked.

The night passed in a blur of champagne, conversations with people whose names I couldn't remember and a growing sense of feeling at ease with Alex. I had almost forgotten that one of the reasons for being here was to meet his parents, when I heard Alex say, 'Mum, Dad, I'd like you to meet Kate.' I almost choked on the champagne I had just sipped.

'Kate, darling, so lovely to finally meet you,' his mother said embracing me in a warm hug.

'Lovely to meet you too Mrs. Gra...' She interrupted me by holding up her bejewelled hand, which dazzled in the light.

'Darling, please, call me Angela,'

'Lovely to meet you Angela,' I tried once again. She beamed at me.

His father, proffered his hand stiffly. 'Call me Arthur.' He was obviously a man of few words.

'Lovely to meet you Arthur,' I repeated, mentally chiding myself for not being able to think of something more original to say.

'Your home is beautiful,' I tried again, looking from one to the other.

'Thank you Kate, I hope we'll be seeing a lot more of you, around here,' Angela smiled, winking at me.

I simply smiled in response, not knowing what to

say.

'Oh there is Dickie,' Arthur said gesturing with his hand in the direction of a hunched, grey haired old man. 'Please excuse me won't you Kate? It was great to finally meet you.' With that he wandered off in the direction of Dickie. Angela also spotted someone that she simply *had* to talk to immediately so she drifted off as well.

'I hope it wasn't something I said?' I joked, although part of me was anxious that I had offended them in some way.

'Don't be silly. They're always distracted when they're hosting a party. Terrified that some guest will feel ignored. They really were thrilled to meet you Kate,' he said reassuringly, while brushing some hair behind my ear and kissing my lips softly. For the remainder of the night, I stuck by Alex like a limpet to a rock. All too soon he was holding a taxi door open for me, which was waiting to whisk me away back to Clapham. I would love to have stayed over but it might have been a bit awkward in the morning, bumping into his mother or father on the landing. I was lingering by the door, reluctant to get in as it would be the end of our evening.

'Have a lovely Christmas,' I almost whispered, before resigning myself to the fact that I would have to leave.

'Are you comin' or goin'?' the taxi driver said in annoyance.

Unable to delay any longer, I slid into the seat and pulled the door closed.

CHAPTER THIRTY TWO

The next morning, my head throbbed and my dehydrated body was crying out for water. Despite this, I felt in surprisingly good spirits. I had four whole days without work! I hugged myself in glee before deciding that I couldn't delay getting up any longer. I had to pack and drive to my parent's house and I was under strict instructions from my mother not to arrive later than 12.30. She was hosting her annual nibbles and drinks party for our cousins and I knew at this very moment she would be buzzing around, stressing about whether she had enough food. She *always* had enough food. In fact, she generally had enough food for two parties.

Just then my phone buzzed with a text message. I expected it to be my sister wondering if I was on the road yet. Rolling over, I picked up the phone from the floor and smiled when I saw that it was from Alex.

Morning sunshine. I have a big smile on my face today after last night. I hope you're not too hungover!Xx

I quickly replied.

Morning!I am definitely hungover but happy. I had a lovely night. Must hydrate before I hit the road though.Xx

With that, I swung into action. For the next hour, I was in a frenzy of activity. I haphazardly wrapped presents, packed and tried to transform my hungover self into something mum would deem presentable. Eventually I stuffed my suitcase into the back of my car and started the two hour journey. There was no escaping the Christmas tunes on the radio so I decided it was a case of if you can't beat 'em join 'em and it wasn't long before I was singing merrily along, as the

Nurofen seemed to be easing the dull ache in my head.

Two and a half hours, one coffee stop and a phonecall from mum later, I pulled into our drive. I felt a sense of excitement and calmness all at once. Before I could even open the door I could see siswa hurtling towards me.

'Siswa!' she said throwing herself at me as I emerged from the car.

'Siswa!' I said back, joyfully hugging her.

'Come on,' she said taking my hand as we disentangled. 'Mum is driving me crazy!'

As our cousins, aunts and uncles began to arrive, I took on the role of meeter and greeter at the door. It meant that I could generally welcome them, hand them a drink and leave them to their own devices. The advantage was that I could put off having to have the 'what are you up to now?' conversations.

'Liz, Happy Christmas,' I said stepping forward to hug one of my mother's sisters.

'Oh Darling, look at you,' she said holding me by the shoulders and stepping back, looking at me up and down. 'You've gotten so skinny! Are you not eating in the big city? Of course I'm obviously just jealous!' she said winking at me. I had always looked up to Aunt Liz when I was growing up. She had never married but was constantly busy with either her job as a magazine editor or with her hectic social life. I had wanted to be her when I was younger. She had seemed so glamorous and worldly.

'Have a drink,' I said handing her a gin and tonic.

She gratefully took the glass, taking a long drink. 'I think I'm going to need this,' she said nodding in the direction of my dad's only sister, Phyllis. They were polar opposites in everything from appearance to personalities to opinions on practically everything.

Probably the only thing that they did agree on was that they didn't like each other very much.

'I'll come rescue you when I've finished with my door duties. I've promised mum that I won't leave this spot until everyone has arrived and has been handed a drink.'

Sighing, she walked in the direction of the kitchen, no doubt in an attempt to avoid Phyllis. Eventually, everyone had arrived and I had to admit that Mum had done a stellar job. The guests were in great spirits, the house was decorated to perfection and the food was delicious. I decided that I really should try and catch up with everyone and while I was trying to figure out who to approach first, Phyllis beat me to it and she was suddenly standing right in front of me, well into my personal space.

'Kate, you look exhausted. You're *very* pale and...'

'Lovely to see you too Phyllis,' I interrupted.

'Yes, well, I'm just concerned about you dear. Up there in London, dealing with all sorts of criminals. I don't know how you do it. I just don't.'

Before I could get a word in, she was off again.

'How you can represent them and sleep well at night, I just don't know. Remind me again Kate, what if they tell you that they've done it, do you still defend them?' she leaned towards me, her beady green eyes wide.

'Well Phyllis, like I've told you before, if a client says that he or she has committed the offence, then we advise them that they should plead guilty and gain maximum credit for doing so.'

What about if they don't want to plead guilty?' she asked. 'What happens if they want you to go to trial and represent them?' she pressed.

I sighed. I had been through this with her last year and the year before and probably the year before that as well.

'If they decide that they want to go to trial, they will be putting the prosecution to proof. This means that it's up to the Crown to prove their case. I wouldn't allow the defendant to give evidence in that instance.'

'Oh. So you'd still represent a guilty criminal then?' she said glaring at me with accusing eyes.

The effect of one too many Sherries was beginning to hit her. My eyes darted around the room, desperately looking for someone to save me. I knew that this conversation was probably heading in the same direction as last year. Her cheeks were flushed and she seemed intent on having a go at me.

Suddenly Uncle Richard appeared by our sides. 'Is Phyllis giving you hard time about your job again?' he asked with a twinkle in his eye. He turned towards his wife. 'Someone has to defend them, isn't that right Kate? It's what our justice system is based on.'

I could see that he was warming to his topic. I definitely didn't want to discuss the finer points of my job with him, so in an attempt to change the subject I offered to get fresh drinks for them. Before they could reply, I hurried off.

Finally people began to trickle off and eventually I was closing the door on the last guest. I almost fell against the door in exhaustion.

'Kate, sweetie, your phone is ringing,' my mum's voice called from the kitchen. I got to it just as the ringing stopped. Almost immediately a text came through. *Basil!* I thought in annoyance. What the hell did he want? As I read through the text my eyes widened in amazement.

'Is everything alright Kate?' my mum asked, as she began loading plates into the dishwasher.

'Yes, yes, fine Mum' I said absentmindedly.

Basil had just asked me to cover Central London

Police Station duties on Christmas day. He *knew* I was at home for four days and was two hours outside of London. Why couldn't he get off his fat arse and do it?

Angrily I typed out a curt reply.

'Not in London until after Boxing day. Cannot cover. Days off were agreed by you.'

Within minutes, my phone buzzed with a reply.

Can't you come back earlier?

Was he being serious?

No, it's important for me to spend Christmas with my family. Who's duty is it?

I was curious to know who was slacking off.

Mine. I can't cover.

Seriously?! There was no way that I was covering his duty. Unless..

I'll do it for a full fee for each case.

I knew he would never agree to this but there was no way I was giving up Christmas with my family. If I did and returned to London but didn't get any calls I wouldn't get paid. As it was I saw my family so little that I really valued spending Christmas with them.

He didn't reply which I took to mean, 'no'! I was probably going to suffer his wrath after the Christmas break but really, what more could he do to me.

CHAPTER THIRTY THREE

The Christmas break flew by and all too soon I was in my car, driving back to London. I felt more rested than I had in a long while and that overwhelming sense of exhaustion I had been feeling was gone. However I was dreading going back to work tomorrow. The feeling grew the closer I got to London and by the time I parked outside our house in Clapham, I almost felt like I had never left. As I hauled my suitcase up the drive, I was dreading the cold empty house. Laura wasn't going to be back for another two days. It was eerily quiet, almost as though everyone had abandoned Clapham for Christmas and hadn't returned yet. I turned the key and hurled myself at the door, using just enough force to open it but not enough to end up on the hallway floor.

As I flicked on the light, I gasped. Lying on the mat, under the post box was a single red rose, looking a little wilted, with a white card attached. I stood there frozen for a moment, with the front door gaping open and my hand stuck to the handle of my suitcase. I didn't know what to do. It was obvious that someone had just slipped the rose through the post box, rather than leaving it outside, but the simple fact of it being *inside* my house completely freaked me out. I pushed the door closed and tried taking deep breaths. I stooped to pick up the card. I contemplated throwing this one away as well without reading it but I couldn't help myself from flicking the card over and glancing at the messy scrawl.

Welcome back Kate. I hope you had a lovely Christmas with your family but it's nice to have you home.

I felt so alone. I couldn't phone the police. What could I say to them? They would probably presume that I was being paranoid but something about it all just didn't seem right. I tried to calm my mind and reasoned with myself that there was no indication that I was in danger. It just seemed to be some strange infatuation that someone had with me. At the moment, the only person I suspected of sending me the roses was Shane Reid and what basis did I have for thinking that? I felt addled and confused and I really wanted to be back at home again.

My phone buzzed, breaking the silence. It was text from an unknown number.

Hope you made it back ok?Xx

My heart started beating faster again.

Almost immediately another text buzzed.

Alex,btw, using work blackberry as my phone had an accident with a pint last night!Xx

I pondered whether to tell him about the new rose. I had told him briefly about the previous ones and he seemed to think the same as Nick. He thought that it was certainly Shane and that I should have gone to the police about it. I decided not to tell him over text.

Back safe and sound. Dreading work tomorrow but can't wait to see you the night after ☺Xx

I would love to be able to see him tomorrow night but I was on call. I switched on the TV, hoping that it would distract me. After watching random reality shows for almost an hour, I felt much more relaxed. There was only one thing for it. I picked up the phone and dialled the Indian takeaway. I felt like I needed a treat.

Later that night as I snuggled up in bed, my thoughts weren't on the roses but on work. I knew the majority of England probably felt the same as I did right now. I doubted that many were actually looking forward to going back to work. But, my time at home had made me even more conscious of how I really didn't like what I was doing anymore. I was also very aware that it may not be possible to continue working for that much longer. Not with the cuts that the Ministry of Justice were proposing to bring in. They were going to cut the number of criminal defence firms in the country from 1600 to 400 which meant that very soon, I could find myself without a job. Maybe that could be a good thing? It could force me to do something that I actually really wanted to do. As I drifted off to sleep, thoughts of setting up my own business floated into my mind. How amazing would it be to be my own boss. There wouldn't be the headache of Basil to deal with. My last thought was that I should do the lottery this week. You just never knew.

CHAPTER THIRTY FOUR

The next day I was duty solicitor in court four at City of Westminster Magistrates Court. As I walked into the courtroom that morning, I crossed my fingers that by some small miracle there would only be a few custody cases needing the duty solicitor. I approached the list-caller and I guessed from her harried demeanour that I was hoping in vain.

'Morning, I'm your custody duty today,' I greeted her with a smile. She didn't return it, which didn't bode well.

'Oh, excellent, sign in there,' she said handing me her clipboard. 'We have ten overnighters downstairs. I'm not sure how many need the duty solicitor at the moment.'

My heart sank. Ten! Hopefully some of them would have their own solicitors already.

'I'll check with the cells to see if they know who needs duty or not.' I turned and walked towards the stairs. I was making an effort to use them instead of the lift as it seemed to be the only exercise that I got these days. On the basement floor, I stood behind two other solicitors who had interpreters with them. We were all waiting for one of the Detention officers to let us in. One of the male solicitors pushed the bell impatiently. He had probably been waiting a while. My guess was that there were more prisoners arriving and all the detention officers were occupied booking them in and getting them safely into cells. Eventually the door swung open and we piled into the small space. I waited patiently for the other solicitors to sign in and get a consultation room to speak with their client's. I wasn't in any rush as I was here all day.

Finally it was my turn.

'Morning M'am. Can I help you?' a tall black detention officer asked as he ate what looked like watery porridge from a plastic bowl. It looked disgusting. Trying not to look at it, I stared at the white board, which had a list of all the detainees who were in custody this morning. Beside their name was the police station they had come from and then in red was marked either 'O/S' if they had their own solicitor or 'Duty' if they needed me to represent them.

At the moment it looked like there were three who required duty. I noted down their names, Luca, Hakim and Cojocaru. Luca would need a Polish interpreter and Cojocaru would need a Romanian.

'Are you expecting more to arrive or is everyone here already?' I asked, somewhat hopeful that they wouldn't be expecting anymore.

He stopped gulping back his gloopy breakfast and had a look at the board.

'We haven't had numbers 12, 16 and 18 arrive yet so don't know if they need duty or not. Hakim hasn't arrived either.'

'Okay well I'll go and find interpreters and come back later then.'

As the steel door closed behind me I walked up to the third floor to where the interpreters had to sign in. As I looked at the book I could see that there was a Polish interpreter at court already but no sign of a Romanian one yet. Well if I could just find the Polish interpreter I could get started. I went into courtroom four and bowed slightly at the bench of Magistrates who were listening to a defence advocate mitigate on behalf of a frail pale looking lady with bad skin and lank matted hair. I crouched down beside the prosecutor and handed him the list of names, I had taken down from the board and waited while he shuffled his bundles around looking for the correct papers. Eventually he handed me the papers.

'Thanks,' I whispered, before standing and leaving the courtroom in search of the Polish interpreter. After much searching I found her and we headed back down to the basement level, this time taking the lift as I didn't think it was fair to enforce my new exercise regime on unwilling parties! As we were walking I had a quick look through his papers. Poor guy. It looked as though he was homeless and had been sleeping in Regents Park. For some reason he had gone knocking on the park keeper's front door just before midnight and when it was opened Mr. Luca had fallen into the hallway and passed out. I scanned through the statement given by the park keeper that night which stated that he had been terrified. The police had been called and it had taken four of them to carry him into the police car as he couldn't be roused.He had been in police custody for two days. I wonder could he even remember what had happened or had he been so drunk that he wouldn't have any recollection of the night.

A short while later the interpreter and I were sitting across from Mr. Luca in a consultation room and it was clear that the poor man couldn't remember anything from two nights ago. As I was telling him what had happened he looked sheepish and embarrassed. I ascertained that he had come to London in 2006 to work and had done so until 2011, when he had started drinking heavily. He had lost his job, his home and his wife and had been sleeping rough since then, with occasional nights spent at hostels. I looked at his list of previous convictions and what he said seemed to check out. He had only started offending in 2011 and most of his convictions were either for being drunk and disorderly or public order offences.

I advised him that he should plead guilty to the offence to obtain maximum credit.

'I'm going to ask the Magistrates to fine you for this offence.' The interpreter translated this and I saw his face drop, so I hurriedly went on to explain that as he had spent two nights in custody, I would ask the court to consider this sentence served and as a result he wouldn't have to pay a fine. He smiled, nodding vigorously. He spoke, his voice sounding urgent and sincere. The interpreter translated it as;

'Thank you. Thank you. Tell court I sorry. I not want to be like this.'

'I will Mr. Luca,' I said rising. 'Hopefully we'll get you on as soon as possible and you can be on your way.' Although, he probably wasn't in a rush anywhere. At least it was warm and he had food in here. Before I left the cells I checked to see if Hakim had arrived yet but unfortunately I would have to make another trip down for him as he still wasn't here. The interpreter went to deal with another detainee and I said I would check in with our list caller to let her know that I was ready with Luca.

My day continued in much the same fashion. I spent my time running up and down the stairs, searching for interpreters and waiting for Hakim. I had dealt with all my other duty cases when he finally arrived at 2.30. They had just made it, as three o' clock was generally the cut off time for getting a prisoner from a prison or police station to court.

I signed in downstairs once again and found a consultation room for Hakim and myself. As I waited I began reading through the allegations against him and looked at his previous convictions. For someone who had only turned 18, he had an impressive fifteen pages filled with convictions ranging from robbery, to criminal damage to possession of firearms. The charges against him today were Possession of Cannabis and a much more serious charge of being in possession of a bladed article. The blade had been an eight inch kitchen knife which he had tucked down his trousers at Kings Cross station. I was almost certain that he wasn't going to be leaving here today. This court took a very dim view of youths carrying blades and knives and I guessed that even if he was to plead guilty today he would be looking at a possible 12 weeks in custody.

I looked up as the door on the other side of the room opened and in walked a tall, black youth with hair tied back. He sat in the chair opposite me and just stared. When I had first started practising he was exactly the type of client who would have intimidated me. He sat slouched in the chair with his right hand down his trousers. This kid knew the system and I just needed to tell him straight what his options were.

'Okay Hakim, there are two charges. Possession of Cannabis and Possession of the knife. I'm not overly worried about the drugs but the knife is a very serious charge. It says here that you live in Leicester and are on a tagged curfew to an address up there. Is that correct?'

'Huh,' he said nodding.

'I'm going to take that as a yes,' I said, trying to hide my exasperation. 'What were you doing in London if you had to be back in Leicester for a curfew that evening?'

'I was at the station innit. I was on my way back to Leicester for my curfew.' This was a vast improvement on grunts as a form of communication.

'What are your curfew hours?' I questioned.

'Nine pm 'til seven in the mornin''

I checked his arrest time at Kings Cross. 'It says here that you were arrested at 9.17pm, so you would have been in breach of your curfew anyway, even if you did go back to Leicester that night.'

He looked a little startled that someone would have figured that out.

'Oh,' he was back to monosyllabic responses.

'There will probably be breach proceedings issued in Leicester but this court won't deal with that today, so let's just concentrate on the charges here, ok?' I said tapping his papers which lay on the table in front of me.

'It says that the cannabis was found in your pocket when you were searched on arrest. Do you admit to this?'

'Ya, just, got it today innit, just for personal use.'

This kid was *so* used to being in court that he was emphasising that the drugs were for his own use and that he hadn't been intending on supplying them, which was obviously a far more serious allegation.

'What about the knife then? That was found down your trousers? In interview you answered no comment to all questions but what are you saying about it now?'

'Protection innit. London is more dangerous than Leicester. I need it on the streets.'

There was no way that I was going to tell the Magistrates that he had been carrying the knife for his protection as this would imply that he was intending to use it. This *definitely* wouldn't help his case.

'What were you doing down in London Hakim? Did you make your curfew in Leicester the night before last?'

'I was just visitin' my cousin in London for the day. I thought I was going to be back in Leicester for my curfew.'

I don't think I really wanted to know why he was visiting his cousin. If this was the story, I had a hunch that there was something gang related going on.

'Right Hakim, because you are admitting to being in possession of the knife and the drugs, you should enter a guilty plea to both. You'll get credit for doing this but I think you will probably get a 12 week custodial sentence for being in possession of the knife. They probably won't take any separate action on the drugs.'

His facial expression didn't change. This wasn't a shock to him. He had been expecting this.

'Do you have any questions for me Hakim?'

'Nah miss.'

I spent another few minutes taking some personal details from him, which I could use for his mitigation, although I suspected that once the Magistrates heard the charges they would be flicking through their sentencing guideline manuals to find out how long they could send him away for.

I finally left court at 6.15 feeling weary and exhausted. As I walked through the sliding glass doors, leaving the stuffy warmth for the chilled December evening, my phone buzzed in my pocket. I pulled the phone out just as it stopped ringing. It had been a blocked number. My initial thought was that it was the call centre with a duty case for me, but then I remembered that I wasn't on duty until 11 that night. Just as I was about to put the phone back in my pocket it started ringing again. I hesitated before answering it. Feeling a sudden annoyance at myself for acting scared, I pressed the answer button.

'Hello?'

I was about to hang up when an automated voice started speaking.

'You are about to receive a call from HMP Thameside. If you do not wish to receive this call please hang up. If you do not wish to receive any future calls like this please call 020 7982 3767. If you wish to receive this call please wait on the line.'

I hesitated momentarily. I never handed out my personal number to clients. How had whoever this was gotten hold of my number? Well if the person was locked up, I presumed that he was disgruntled, so I prepared myself for either abuse or pleas to get him out.

There was a click as the call was connected. I stayed silent and waited for them to speak first.

'Hello?' a quiet male voice said.

'Hi, can I help you?' I said in reply.

'Is this Kate Hunter?' the voice asked, sounding more self assured now.

'Yes, who is calling?' I was tired and hungry and really not in the mood for a pissed off client.

'Doesn't matter. I wanted to warn you. You need to be careful.'

The line went dead. He had hung up. I stood still, staring at the phone in my hand, as busy commuters rushed passed me. I felt dazed and stepped back towards the courthouse to get out of peoples way. There were so many thoughts and questions running through my mind.

Who was this person who had just phoned? Surely there was a way I could check the prison phone records? What did he mean when he said I needed to be careful? Was this connected to the roses I had been getting? It seemed logical that it was.

Suddenly I felt overwhelmed and desperately needed to talk about this with someone. I looked at the phone in my hand, as though I expected it to tell me who I should contact. There was no point calling Siswa because she would just worry too much. The same went for either of my parents. My best bet was someone who already knew about the roses and phone calls from blocked numbers. My fingers jumped into action.

Laura are you about tonight? I really need someone to talk to about something?

I hit send before I could change my mind.

Defo. I'll get us an Indian. My ears are all yours. XX

I breathed a sigh of relief and I could feel my

shoulders relax a little. I didn't feel as alone anymore.

CHAPTER THIRTY FIVE

'Fudge it Kate, you can't just ignore the call,' Laura said, as she ripped off a piece of naan bread. I had to admire how she was sticking with this not cursing thing.

'I mean, whoever it was wouldn't have bothered calling as a prank, would they?' She paused, looking thoughtful as she dipped the bread in some chutney. 'Do you know which prison Shane Reid was in most recently? You could find that out, couldn't you, even if you didn't know?'

I nodded miserably. 'He was in HMP Thameside. I think he was only released a couple of months ago. He did a bit of a stretch there, over a year I think.'

Laura's face lit up. 'There you have it!' she exclaimed, casting her hand towards me. 'Shane obviously told someone at HMP Thameside that he's obsessed with you and ..' she trailed off.

'What were you going to say Laura?' I asked, even though I had a feeling I knew what it was.

'Well,' she hesitated before continuing. 'He obviously has some sort of plan which he is carrying out. Maybe he came up with it while he was inside and told whoever called you today.'

'I just don't understand why he didn't tell me who he was or why I needed to be careful. Why was he so cryptic? He literally just said three short sentences and hung up.'

'I don't know. Maybe there's some code among prisoners. What goes on inside stays inside? Perhaps he felt that you should be warned but at the same time he didn't want to be seen as a grass.'

We both ate in silence for a few minutes, considering everything that we had just discussed.

'God your work is *so* much more exciting that mine,' Laura exclaimed, breaking the silence. 'The most excitement I ever get is an all nighter reading contracts. Here you have a real-life stalker!' She saw the look on my face. 'Sorry,' she said. 'I was only trying to make you feel better. It is pretty awful. The question now is what are you going to do about it?'

The question hung in the air between us. Could I go to the police now with what we had just deduced? Or would it make any difference if I did? What evidence did I have to prove that it was Shane? I didn't have anything tangible. They would be able to trace the call from HMP Thameside to my phone and then check the phone records in the prison to figure out who had made the call. But the likelihood of whoever had made the call actually giving evidence against someone he had served time with was minimal.

'Kate, you have to tell the police,' she said emphatically. 'This phonecall takes it to a whole other level.'

'Do you really think so?' I asked

'Kate,' Laura said with an element of frustration in her voice. '*Of Course* you have to tell the police. You deal with dangerous people every day of the week. You know better than most people, what they are capable of. You said yourself that they can be the nicest people in the world to you but when you read through their papers you can see the horrendous things that they are capable of doing.

I knew that she was right. I also knew that there was very little the police would probably do, other than log the complaint.

'Ok, you're right,' I conceded. 'I'll do it tomorrow.'

Laura looked happier now and I had to admit that I did feel slightly better.

'So,' I said, sounding much cheerier than I had previously. 'Tell me all about your Christmas. Did you see Dave when you were at home?' I asked, wiping my plate clean with the last remaining piece of Naan bread.

It was nice to be able to focus on something other than someone possibly trying to do me harm and listening to Laura's voice as she recounted a particularly awkward meeting between her ex Dave and his current girlfriend, at the local pub was exactly what I needed. After a while my phone rang, interrupting her flow of chat. We both stared at eachother, our eyes wide. My arm stretched out to grab it from the coffee table. I checked the screen. It was a blocked number. I showed it to Laura. The phone continued to buzz. I answered it, putting the phone on speaker, so as Laura could hear what would be said, or not said.

'Good evening, this is the Defence Solicitors Call Centre, Candice speaking. I have a rota matter. Are you available to take the details?' a Geordie voice boomed out pleasantly. I almost burst out laughing. I had totally lost track of the time and I could see now from glancing at Laura's watch that it was 11.15pm. I had been on call since eleven.

'Hi, yes. This is Miss Hunter, pin number 12987 . Just give me a moment please while I grab a pen.'

'Certainly Miss Hunter, take your time.'

As I searched around for a pen and paper I took the call off speaker so as the lady on the other end couldn't hear Laura who was rolling around on the floor laughing hysterically.

'Okay I'm ready,' I said my pen poised over the piece of paper I had pulled from under the couch. I was trying my hardest not to laugh.

'Ok Miss Hunter, we have an adult female at West End Central Police Station. Her name is Vera Lopez. There for the offence of dwelling burglary. I have a note that says a Spanish interpreter will be required. The reference is 100897656A. Do you need any more details?'

'Do you have the custody number?'

'Certainly. It's 8456. Anything else I can do for you Miss Hunter?'

'No that's everything, thank you.'

'Sorry!' Laura gasped, after I had hung up. 'I couldn't help it. I think it was the build up of tension in my body finding a release.'

She began clearing up the remains of our dinner from the coffee table as I phoned the Police station to find out what was going on with Ms. Lopez. The line was busy so I decided to wash my face and brush my teeth and try again in a little while. Hopefully they wouldn't be ready to interview her tonight and I might actually get a good night's sleep.

As I brushed my teeth, my phone buzzed again. Hurriedly I spat out and wiped my mouth before answering the phone. I had another case at West End Central Police station. This time it was a male adult, Akwasi Ufi who had been arrested for robbery. After getting all the details I needed I tried the police station again. Still engaged.

I decided to get into my pyjamas. I knew from experience that this was just tempting fate and that the likelihood was that I would have to get dressed again and head to the station but for once I just wanted to be wrong about it. Once I was all bundled up in bed, I tried the station again. This time it started ringing. My guess was the station was extremely busy as it seemed to ring forever before someone answered it.

'Hello, custody West End Central,' a breathless female voice said. 'Sorry,' she added, 'we've just had a bit of a situation here. I just need to catch my breath.'

'No problem, take your time.'

'Right, so how can I help you?' she asked when she had recovered sufficiently to talk without keeling over.

'I'm duty solicitor tonight. I'm making first calls for two clients.' I gave her the names and crossed my fingers as she gave me the details on them that I wouldn't have to go out tonight. I stifled a yawn as I gave her my name, firm name and contact details.

'Have officers been appointed to deal with the cases?' I enquired.

'Let me just look,' she paused for a moment and I could hear the tapping of her keyboard as she logged into relevant files. 'At the moment it says here that Lopez will need an interpreter and Ufi does have an OIC appointed. I can give you his contact number and you can contact him directly if you like?'

'Yes, please,' I said as I jumped out of bed and went in search of a pen. After hanging up, I resumed my working position of being once again bundled up under my duvet. I dialled the Officers number and for about the fifth time that night crossed my fingers that they wouldn't be ready for interview until the morning. The really annoying thing though about all these calls was that I wouldn't get paid for them if I didn't attend the police station interview tonight. As tomorrow was a normal weekday, I wouldn't get paid 'out of hours' for attending the station.

'Hello, DC Chambers speaking,'

'Hi, this is Miss Hunter, the solicitor for Ufi calling. I wanted to check what the situation with your investigation was and whether you had an idea of when the interview was going to be.'

'Oh Hello, Miss Hunter. Well at the moment we've just got authorisation to do a s18 search and we also have CCTV footage to view so, at this stage I think that the interview will be in the morning.'

I breathed a sigh of relief. Although I could have

done with the extra money, all I really wanted right now was to get some sleep.

'Ok, thank you, I'll be in touch in the morning so to find out the situation,' I said before hanging up. I phoned custody back and asked to speak with the client. We had one of those useless conversations, where his English was so accented that I couldn't understand him. Finally at almost 1.45am, when I could barely keep my eyes open any longer, I switched off my light. Then when my brain was no longer occupied, I started to think of the phonecall I had received earlier and it wasn't long before I was so tense again that sleep seemed an impossibility.

After about an hour of tossing and turning, my phone began to ring. I groaned and reached for it.

'Hello this is the Defence Solicitors Call Centre, are you available to take a rota case?' I sighed and suddenly felt exhausted again.

CHAPTER THIRTY SIX

Thirty minutes later, I was dressed and in the kitchen making some coffee to take with me to Charing Cross station. There was fourteen year old girl in custody who had been arrested for assault and they would be ready to interview her at 4am. It was her first time being arrested and they were eager to interview her, given her age. Well at least I'd get one fee out of the night I thought, trying to look on the bright side.

As I headed out into the cold night, I cupped the travel mug with my hands, trying to warm them up. It was *so* quiet and I began to feel uneasy as I rummaged around in my bag for my car keys. I heard footsteps on the other side of the road and I became frantic, anxiously peering into my bag in the dimly lit street. I tried my coat pockets and felt a surge of relief course through me as I found them in my left pocket. Just then the lady who lived beside us crossed the road, with her dog on a lead. Dog walking at 4am? Really? I nodded at her before diving into the car and putting on the auto lock.

I hastily started the engine and began to drive, faster than I should have done towards the station. For probably the first time ever I felt relieved to enter the police station in the middle of the night. It felt safe. I phoned through to custody to let them know I was here and sat down on a blue metal chair to wait. Twenty minutes later I was still waiting so decided to ring through to custody again.

'Sorry Miss,' a voice at the other end of the line said before I had the chance to say hello.

'We've had a bit of an incident here. A detainee smuggled in a blade and tried to commit suicide in his cell. We've got it under control now and officer in your case will be with you shortly.'

'Ok thank you,' I said before returning to my metal chair to wait. Sure enough a few minutes later an officer poked his head through the door.

'Miss Hunter?'

I stood, eager to get going, although I really wasn't in a huge rush as I had already ruled out sleep tonight.

'Yes, I'm here for the case of Lynda Mehmet.'

'Lovely, come right through. Sorry about the delay, I think the Detention Seargent told you the reason?'

'Yes, it sounds awful. Is he going to be alright?'

'Honestly we're not sure at this point. He's been transferred to the hospital but there was an awful lot of blood. His cell is a complete bloodbath.'

Unsure of how to respond I stayed silent.

I went through the motions of handing my business card to the custody sergeant, getting the custody record and eventually disclosure about the allegation from the Officer. While I waited for Lynda to be brought into the consultation room, I tried to stay occupied by getting started on my paperwork. I looked up as the door opened and a pale fragile looking girl entered. She looked terrified and cold. She was dressed in grey tracksuit pants and a white string top. Before I even introduced myself I asked the Officer for a blanket which she could wrap around herself. The officer nodded before closing the door behind him. I ran through the basics of introducing myself and explaining that she had the right to free and independent legal advice while she was in custody. She nodded occasionally, presumably to indicate that she understood, but she still hadn't spoken. As I read out the allegation to her, I could see her body twitching. She looked eager to get her side of the story across.

The allegation was one of assault and the victim was also a girl of fourteen who claimed that Lynda followed her as she left school and started yelling at her. She then claimed that Lynda pushed her and when she fell to the floor that Lynda continued to punch her with a closed fist.

'Well, see it's like this,' Lynda began breathlessly, anxious to get her side across.

'I did do it, but see there's a reason.' Her eyes welled up with tears. I bet there's a boy involved I thought to myself.

'She's a slag. She was putting stuff on facebook about things she had been doing with my boyfriend.' I rooted around in my handbag to see if I could find a tissue, as she began crying. The officer picked that moment to knock and open the door with a large blue blanket in his hands. Lynda wrapped it around her shoulders, taking comfort in its warmth.

'Lynda would you like a break? Or I can get you some water or tea if you'd like?'

She sniffled again, shaking her head. 'I'm ok,' she said quietly.

'Do you feel well enough to continue telling me what happened?'

She nodded. 'I did follow her. I wanted to ask her why she had gone off with my boyfriend. Then when I saw her I was so angry,' she said emphatically. I stayed silent, noting down what she was saying, hoping that she would continue without prompting.

'She wasn't sorry for what she had done at all. She was smiling and saying how great it had been, so I hit her across the face and she fell to the floor. I hit her again and then she pulled my hair and we ended up scrapping.'

'Do you go to the same school as her?' I interrupted.

'No, I don't go to school anymore. I dropped out last year. I was picking my little sister up from school and I saw Chantelle coming out of the gates and I couldn't help myself.'

'Are you still with your boyfriend?' I asked more out of curiosity than anything else.

'No,' she replied softly, her eyes welling up again. 'I took an overdose when we split up and ended up in hospital. Then he called me a psycho.'

'Oh Lynda, you deserve better than him,' I said feeling a pang of sympathy for her. 'Do you live with your parents?' I asked, thinking that I already knew the answer.

'Foster mum. I never knew my dad and my mum left me alone one day in the house and never came back.'

My heart went out to her but I knew that all I could do was try and get the best result possible for her today and then she would go back to her life. She pulled the blanket tighter around her shoulders and shivered. She was eager to get on with it now and hopefully get out of the station as soon as possible. I went through her interview options with her, explaining everything in depth as it was her first time being interviewed.

'So my advice to you,' I concluded, 'is to explain fully to the officer what happened. I'm almost 100 per cent positive that you'll get a reprimand for this matter and that will be the end of it. Do you want me to explain what a reprimand is?'

'No, my friend got one. I know what it is. I have to go to the Youth Offending Team and they give out to me for a bit but then I don't have to come back to the station at all.'

I smiled. That was more or less it.

'Well, if you feel ready for your interview, I can get the officer. Unfortunately your foster mother wasn't able to attend for the interview so the police have contacted a social worker who will sit in and act as an appropriate adult. He or she is only there because you

244

are a youth and their job is to ensure that you understand everything that goes on during the interview. Is that okay?'

She nodded, seemingly unperturbed that her foster mother couldn't be bothered to come to the station for her interview. She reminded me of a little dog who had been kicked one too many times and didn't have expectations anymore, even of people who were supposed to care for her.

CHAPTER THIRTY SEVEN

At 6.30am I left the station, feeling exhausted and wondering if any of the coffee shops around were open yet. Unfortunately they all appeared to be closed for business so I hopped in my car and drove back to Clapham. I longed for a warm shower and strong coffee. As much as I wanted to crawl back into bed, I would have to do a quick turn around and come back to the station to deal with the other two calls I got last night. My Christmas break seemed like a distant memory.

As I parked, I could see the light on in Laura's bedroom. No doubt she would be rushing out the door in a few minutes. I fell into the hallway, thinking that we really had to get onto Bob about the door. I could smell burnt toast and Laura was waving a tea towel around frantically, no doubt in an effort to get some of the smoke to dissipate. Fixing the fire alarm was another thing I could add to Bob's list.

'Sorry, sorry!' Laura said absentmindedly, as she slipped some fresh bread in to the toaster.

'Toast?' she asked.

'No, I'm okay. I think I need to wash first and drink some very strong coffee.'

'Rough night?' Laura asked while she searched around in the packed condiment cupboard.

'Same, same but different,' I replied with a weary smile. 'If you're looking for the marmalade we're out of it.'

'Fudge it. I'll get some food on my way back from work this evening. You'd think a pair of students lived here!'

I trudged up the stairs to shower and stared at myself in the mirror, marvelling at how tired I looked. I turned away. This job was aging me. As I stood under the hot shower, I took some deep breaths and steeled myself for the day ahead. I really didn't know how I was going to be in any fit shape for a date with Alex tonight.

After dressing, downing two strong coffees and feeling only slightly more awake I pulled the front door closed behind me and walked towards the tube station. Just as I was about to head underground with a copy of the Metro my phone started buzzing. After fishing it out from the bottom corner of my handbag I saw 'blocked number' flashing on the screen. After a moment's hesitation I answered it.

'Good morning, Kate Hunter speaking.' I waited, somewhat anxiously, for a response.

'Oh good morning Miss Hunter, this is DC Wiggans from West End Central Police Station. I believe you are dealing with Akwasi Ufi?'

'Yes, that's right.'

'We're going to be ready to interview him in an hour. Would you be in a position to attend the station at 9.30?'

'Yes, that's no problem. I'll be there then.' I took a few more details from her and hung up. I decided I would check on my other client Vera Lopez when I got there.

About forty five minutes later I was climbing the steps to West End Central Station, grasping a coffee cup with an extra shot in my hand. DC Wiggans appeared through the doors at 9.30 on the dot. I stood, ready to walk through to the custody centre with her.

'Miss Hunter?' she enquired looking at me.

'Hi, yes,' I confirmed.

'We've had a bit of a development. We're not actually ready for interview yet I'm afraid. I've just had a section 18 search authorised and officers have left to search Mr. Ufi's house. I did try to reach you but I imagine you were on the tube because the call wouldn't connect.

If this had been on my own time during out of hours I would have been annoyed but as it was a normal working day I just took it in my stride.

'Ok, no problem. I have another client here so perhaps I could go through with you to the custody suite and check on the status of that case?'

'Sure, no problem. Just follow me.'

As I trailed after her, my phone began to ring again. It was another blocked number. Hopefully this is the OIC from my other case saying they're ready to go, I thought to myself.

'Hello, Kate Hunter speaking,' I answered, waiting for the voice of a police officer to speak.

There was silence. I checked the phone. Sometimes there was a poor signal in here but my screen said that there was full coverage. I tried again.

'Hello? Hello?'

There was only silence. I felt a chill run through my body.

'Don't hang up,' a distorted sounding voice, broke through the silence. All sorts of thoughts were running through my head. It sounded like whoever was speaking was using something to distort the sound of his voice. Surely that could only mean that I knew them and they were afraid I would recognise their voice. I waited for the person to speak again. Despite being in one of the safest places I felt scared. There was a crackle on the line and the voice spoke again.

'Don't be scared Kate. I saw you this morning and you seemed terrified. There's no need to be afraid. I simply want to spend time with you.'

My brain was whirring. I needed to use this

248

opportunity to try and find out who was leaving the roses. Moreover he was following me. Was he outside right now? I felt panicked.

'Who are you?' I asked in a shaky voice. I was alone in the corridor, as the OIC had continued to wherever she needed to be. I didn't know if this was the right thing to ask but what else could I say.

'You know who I am Kate.' The way he said my name sounded so threatening.

'Shane?' I whispered.

Silence. Then the phone went dead.

'Miss are you okay?' a passing officer asked, looking at me with concern. I was leaning against the wall using it for support.

I took a deep breath. 'Yes, thank you. I'm fine. Just too much caffeine,' I tried to joke, with a wan smile.

'If you're sure?' he said uncertainly.

'I'm just on my way to the custody suite,' I said trying to reassert myself. 'I have a client in custody and need to find out the status regarding interview times.'

He seemed to relent. 'I'll buzz you through shall I?'

'Thank you,' I said weakly as I followed him down the hallway. What should I do? Tell the police? It seemed to be the only option really. I didn't have any proof that it was Shane. It was only suspicion on my part, but I could at least tell them about the phone calls and the roses. Having decided that this is what I would do, I felt more relaxed and I could feel some of the tension leave my body. I entered the custody suite which looked busy but under control.

There were two men being booked in. Both looked homeless and as I got nearer I could smell that they probably were. Both were in need of a haircut and a good wash. The way they were joking with the officers suggested that they were regulars in here and weren't overly bothered about having to spend time in police custody. In fact it was probably a relief to get to spend some time in a warm environment where they could be assured some food.

Just then I got a text from Basil.

Where r u? We have someone who is being bought over to City of Westminster Magistrates Court this afternoon. Can you attend?

Where did he think I was? I wondered in irritation. He always checked with the call centre the morning following our duties to make sure that we had answered all the calls. He knew full well that I was here.

West End Central PS. Covering cases I got last night. Doubt I'll be finished by lunch time

I breathed out through gritted teeth. He *really* annoyed me.

I'm sending Emily to cover your cases at West End Central. Please can you cover City of Westminster this afternoon. I'll email you the details.

Usually I would be thrilled to get to leave a police station for court but today I felt somewhat cocooned here. This feeling of safety had calmed my nerves and the thought of having to leave made me feel anxious. I let the custody sergeant know that my colleague would be dealing with the clients from now on and asked for a door release to be let out. As I walked out into the reception area, I decided that there was no time like the present and that I should lodge my complaint here.

I went through the procedure that hundreds of other Londoners undergo every day. I answered the questions put to me by the officer as best I could, while all the time suspecting that the complaint would be left on a shelf to gather dust.

'Alright love,' the officer who took my complaint said. 'If you can think of anything else that might help us, dial this number,' he said as he scrawled something on a piece of paper. He passed it to me and smiled kindly.

'Is there anything else I can help you with?' he questioned, obviously ready to dismiss me and my fears.

'No. I suppose that's everything. Thank you,' I said as I backed away from the counter. I went to the metal chairs and took a few moments to tidy my bag and wrap my coat tighter around me. Eventually I couldn't think of a reason to delay any longer and I walked through the sliding doors into the January chill. I looked around fearfully. Was he here now? Was he watching? Feeling grateful for the bright day and the fact that I was in busy central London, I checked the time. I decided that I could get an early lunch and then head to City of Westminster.

CHAPTER THIRTY EIGHT

At 4.30 that afternoon, I sat tiredly in Courtroom five, waiting for my case to be called on. I stifled a yawn, not wanting the bench to think I was bored. Although of the three Magistrates, two of them definitely looked zoned out and I doubted they would have noticed if I had fallen asleep.

I had spent a frustrating hour this afternoon trying to track down an Urdu interpreter and then a further hour trying to explain to my client that beating his wife was wrong, under English law. He fully admitted that he did it but couldn't understand why it was a matter that the police should get involved in. Eventually he seemed to understand that if he pleaded guilty today he would get a reduced sentence. Apparently his brother, Amjad was going to allow him to be bailed to his address. If he was granted bail he certainly wouldn't be allowed to return to his home address because his wife lived there.

I was jolted back to the present by the list-caller calling on my case.

'Next on your list is Mr. Yasir Rizvi, represented by Miss. Hunter.' I gathered my papers and moved up a bench so as I was sitting to the left of the Prosecutor.

'Good afternoon, your Worships,' I greeted them, bowing slightly.

They nodded tiredly at me.

'Any indication on plea?' the legal clerk whispered.

'Guilty plea and bail app,' I stage whispered back. Satisfied with this, she sat back in her chair and began to get a head start on inputting the information from this case into her system. I leafed through my notes as I waited for Yasir to be bought up from the cells. Eventually he was lead by two detention officers into the small box like area which was screened by glass.

The list caller let the interpreter into this area and he swore an oath to interpret the truth and only the truth.

Yasir entered a guilty plea and I asked the court to adjourn the matter so as reports on him could be prepared by the probation service before sentencing. A date for sentencing was fixed and then the issue of bail needed to be decided. As he had already entered a guilty plea, the Prosecution weren't in a position to object to bail. However the court usually allowed them to provide their observations on the issue of bail, which to me seemed to be the same thing. The crowns observations in this case were that he would further offend if he was released on bail.

When it was my turn to argue on behalf of Yasir, I submitted that he should be admitted on bail with conditions attached. I put forward the brother's address and proposed that he should have to live and sleep at this address.

'A further condition, your worships, which would go towards satisfying yourselves that he couldn't further offend would be to put a condition in place that he not contact directly or indirectly his wife. Also a condition that he not go to his home address could be put in place.'

I went on to say that he worked in an electrics shop and if he were to be remanded, he would lose his job and as a result would be in difficulty paying his rent which would have repercussions for his wife and two children. I concluded by saying that although he did have previous convictions on his record he had never failed to surrender to the courts so there was no form to suggest that he wouldn't turn up for his sentencing on this occasion.

I sat down, and the Magistrates huddled closer together, with their heads bowed, whispering and trying to make a decision. The prosecution hadn't mentioned that his wife wanted a restraining order put in place so it was my guess that Yasir would be back at home sooner rather than later. The Magistrates finally raised their heads and the chairman began to speak.

'We have carefully considered everything Miss Hunter has said on your behalf Mr. Rizvi. We have also taken the observations of the Prosecution on board. We have decided that you can be released on bail with conditions attached.'

She went on to list the conditions I had proposed in my bail application.

'If you breach any of those conditions you will have breached your bail and may very well find yourself back in police custody and indeed back before us again. Do you understand?' she asked looking at Yasir.

He nodded.

'Alright, that is all. You will be released shortly. I'm sure your lawyer will want a word with you downstairs before you leave.' With that she looked at the list caller to move onto the next case. I stood and bowed slightly and as I left my spot another lawyer moved in to occupy it.

The interpreter and I went downstairs to the cells to make sure that Yasir understood exactly what had happened in court. Once again I had to explain to him that until he was sentenced he couldn't go near his wife. Despite having explained all this earlier and having agreed the bail conditions with him, he seemed completely put out by the fact that he couldn't see his wife. He clearly viewed her as his property. He eventually reluctantly nodded his head and said that he would comply with his bail conditions.

After leaving the cells, I walked quickly up two flights of stairs to the advocate's room. I couldn't wait to leave this building. The room was pretty quiet except for a couple of barristers having a heated conversation at the other end of the room about the state of the profession. After eavesdropping for a few minutes I gathered that one of them was actually a solicitor.

'Overnight we could all be unemployed!' he exclaimed. 'I can't believe that they want to reduce the number of defence firms in it this country by so much. It's just crazy. Even if my firm was lucky enough to be one of the 400 which would be granted a contract, I'd be working for peanuts. No! Not peanuts. Peanut shells!'

He was really warming to his topic now. I slowed down putting my papers into my bag so as I could continue listening. He was voicing the concerns of solicitors in every part of the country.

'What is it they say?' he continued. 'Pay peanuts and you get monkeys working for you.' It looked as though the other man wanted to butt in and say something but the man I had guessed was a solicitor was on a roll.

'And to pay us the same fees regardless if a client pleads guilty at the first hearing or if we have to go to trial on it is utterly ludicrous. I just can't get my head around it at all,' he spluttered. 'It will wipe us out overnight!' he said gesturing with his hand for emphasis.

'I agree Nigel,' his friend managed to interject. 'It will take away the right of a defendant to choose his or her own lawyer. As ridiculous as that sounds, it will mean people will be arrested by the state, prosecuted by the state, defended by the state and sentenced by the state.'

Not wanting to be outdone, his friend chimed in. 'Preposterous!' he exclaimed.

Having heard enough, I slipped on my flats, put my heels in my bag and left the room. I couldn't bear to listen to anymore of what I already knew too well. I walked down the stairs, feeling drained but happy to be almost finished for the day. I knew that I wouldn't have time to get back home and change before my dinner date with Alex. I looked down at my black boring suit. There was nothing I could do to jazz this up, I sighed. As much as I wanted to see him, I also just wanted to roll into bed. Suddenly the thought of rolling into bed with Alex entered my mind and the butterflies which seemed only to appear when I thought of him, surfaced in my stomach.

A little while later, I barged into the room I shared with Nick. Always predictable, Nick had his feet up on his desk and was attempting the crossword.

'Have you ever completed that thing?' I asked in greeting.

'Hello to you too!' he replied with a smile. 'Coffee? Tea? I'm going to make some and I may even be able to rummage up some chocolate biscuits,' he said with a wink. Chocolate was always my weakness, particularly when I was tired.

'How can I refuse? A tea would be lovely. Thanks Nick.'

While Nick went to the kitchen, I busied myself turning on my computer and trying to arrange the bundle of paperwork which lay on my desk into some type of order.

Nick, entered the room a few moments later, balancing a tray in one hand and a packet of biscuits in the other.

'Just a thought Nick but why didn't you put the biscuits on the tray?'

'Well m'lady I didn't want any of the chocolate melted by the hot teacups.'

'Ah so there is method to your madness!' I exclaimed.

'You of little faith,' he muttered. 'You look shattered Kate,' he said as he handed me a cup of tea. Black and not too strong, just how I liked it.

Just then a text came through on my phone.

Kate I'm SO sorry. I've literally just been landed with a 2 day trial starting tomorrow. I'm not going to be able to make dinner tonight☹. I'll have to spend most of the night drinking coffee and prepping it.Xx

Part of me felt deflated. I had been really looking forward to seeing Alex as I hadn't seen him since the party at his parent's house.

'Is that from Alex?' Nick enquired.

'Are you psychic now?' I joked.

'I was just reading your facial expressions. Ha! No I'm definitely not that intuitive with girls, as my girlfriend keeps telling me. I know you were supposed to have dinner with Alex tonight. I tried to get him to cover a case for me tomorrow at Highbury Magistrates Court but his Clerk said that he was going to be involved in a two day trial, but didn't know it yet. I just guessed that he was texting to cancel because he would have to prep it tonight.'

'Ah so not psychic at all then,' I smiled.

'I'm glad you said that though,' I admitted. 'Part of me was wondering if he was making it up as an excuse not to see me.'

'Oh I wouldn't worry about that,' Nick said. 'Alex is totally into you.'

I couldn't help blushing, which made Nick laugh at me.

'Hi Nick,' Emily said over enthusiastically, as she wandered into the room. 'Hi Kate,' she said with a fraction of the enthusiasm.

'Thanks for landing me with your work today Kate,' she said icily. 'It's not like I haven't got other more important things to do.'

Like spending your daddy's money I thought to myself. Biting my tongue I replied as civilly as I could manage. 'Basil's instructions Emily. Nothing to do with me.'

'Emily if you don't mind, Kate and I are having an important chat about a case we're running together. I don't mean to be rude but we need to get it sorted out tonight.' Nick said with a smile.

I could have hugged him.

'Emily looked affronted but instead replied politely, 'Of course you do. I'll chat to you tomorrow Nick,' she said, leaving the room without making any attempt to say good bye to me.

I rolled my eyes at Nick. 'Thank you,' I whispered.

'No problem. I can't stand her fawning. Anyway there was something I did want to talk to you about. Did you go to the police about the roses and phone calls you've been getting?'

I nodded, taking a sip of the hot tea. There was something very soothing about a cup of tea.

'I was at West End Central today and before I left I made a complaint to the police. You know as well as I do though that it's probably going to be put on a shelf and forgotten about.'

Nick sat back looking thoughtful. 'Have you had any more unwanted phonecalls or roses?'

I hesitated, reluctant to replay the phonecall I had received earlier. Nick knew me too well to try and fob him off.

'Kate?' he said with an edge in his voice.

I relented and recounted what had happened earlier. He looked more and more serious as I spoke. In fact it was unnerving seeing him like this. When I finished he seemed momentarily lost for words.

Finally he seemed to come to life. 'Kate this is ridiculous,' he spluttered. 'I can't believe you aren't taking this more seriously. Someone is bloody stalking you for christsake. I'm telling Basil right now,' he said standing.

'Nick no, please,' I pleaded. 'You know that Basil doesn't like me and he makes my life difficult enough as it is. I really don't want to draw him on me any more than I have to.'

Nick paused and seemed to be considering what I had said.

'Kate, you don't seem to be looking at this clearly. You've had warnings from someone inside prison for God's sake. Wake up!'

He looked mad. I just stared at him, too stunned to speak. I'd never seen Nick seem so perturbed. Silently I nodded my head.

'Okay,' I said softly. Suddenly I felt overwhelmed and exhausted and I just wanted someone to tell me what to do.

'Come on,' he said determinedly.

I gulped back the last of my tea and followed him out of our office and down the corridor to Basil's room. Nick rapped on the door, while I stood silently behind him, mentally preparing myself for the conversation I didn't want to have. I knew from working with Basil that he would do anything to keep a client on side, particularly with all the new threatened cuts. There was silence on the other side of the door. Usually we would have been met with a yell by this point.

'I wonder where he is?' Nick mused out loud.

'Emily?' he shouted down the corridor. 'Do you know where Basil is?'

Always eager to speak to Nick, Emily appeared at her door with amazing speed. Her beaming smile dropped once she saw me.

'He's gone to a conference on Best Value Tendering. He won't be back for today. Can I help you with anything?'

'No, no, thanks,' Nick said distractedly. 'Dammit,' he muttered and walked back to our office. I followed behind like a shadow.

'First thing tomorrow we have to talk to Basil Kate,' he said as he sat down in the chair opposite me. Before I could say anything his phone buzzed. He glanced at it and made an apologetic face at me. 'Sorry Kate, it's the girlfriend. I'm going to have to go. Apparently it's vital that I help her shop for the drinks for the new year's party we're throwing tomorrow night.' He almost grimaced. 'You should come? If you don't have plans?'

'I think I'm doing something with Alex actually,' I said shyly.

'Ooh ringing in the New Year together,' he said with a smile. 'Serious stuff!'

I was grateful for the lightened mood. 'Well enjoy the shopping. Apparently 2010 is a good year for Beaujolais,' I said with a smile. 'Now I've just exhausted all my wine knowledge on you!'

'Okay,' Nick said almost reluctantly while he stood and wrapped himself in his coat. 'I've received my orders.' Something about his tone made me feel as though there was trouble in paradise, but I really wasn't in the mood for prying.

'Are you going to be alright?' he asked looking at me in concern.

'Absolutely.' I said with false brightness. 'I'm going to get on top of some of this mountain,' I said tapping the pile of paperwork on my desk and then I'll go home for some much wanted sleep.'

''If you're sure?' Nick asked. I knew he felt torn. He *had* to go and meet Milly but he also felt as though he should ensure I was okay.

'Honestly Nick, I'm fine, enjoy your evening and I'll see you tomorrow.'

CHAPTER THIRTY NINE

After what seemed like an eternity I had managed to get through half of the paperwork on my desk. My eyes were twitching so much that I couldn't ignore them anymore. I decided to call it a night and went through my usual routine of shutting down my prehistoric computer, packing my bag and wrapping myself up against the cold.

As I pulled the door to the building closed, I felt a flutter of fear in my stomach. It was dark and despite the busy streets, I couldn't shake the feeling that someone could be watching me. I marched briskly towards the tube station.

After a completely ordinary journey, I emerged from Clapham Common tube station, cold, tired and hungry. I stuffed my hands in my pockets and decided that it was definitely a night for a takeaway. I pulled my phone from my pocket and quickly ordered my usual as I walked.

'Thank you miss, that will be with you within 45 minutes,' the all too familiar voice said.

As I reached our drive I saw the lights on inside. I hadn't realised Laura was going to be home tonight and felt a twinge of guilt for not phoning her to see if she wanted an Indian. I could always phone again if she did I decided as I inserted my key in the door. I threw my bodyweight against it and tumbled into the hallway. There was a delicious smell wafting from the direction of the kitchen. Laura must be cooking one of her Bali inspired dishes, I thought, my guilt at not having thought of her before I ordered easing.

'I'm home!' I singsonged. I felt a sense of calm which I hadn't felt since I had been at my parent's home for Christmas.

'Mmm, something smells delicious.' There was no reply. I had never known her to be so engrossed in cooking. I locked the front door behind me and headed upstairs to change out of my suit. Feeling more relaxed in my comfy clothes, I headed downstairs and turned on the TV, while I waited for my delivery. I curled up on the couch.

'Kate, you're finally home. I was beginning to get worried,' a voice said from the doorway. A male voice. I froze and slowly turned to my right. I could feel the blood drain from my face and it felt like my heart had stopped beating. It was almost as though I couldn't process the fact that he was standing in front of me in my home.

'Shane?' I whispered. 'What are you doing here?'

'I'm cooking us dinner Kate. Doesn't it smell delicious?' He seemed oblivious to the fact that he had just broken into my house. In fact he was acting as though it was the most normal thing in the world for him to be standing in my sitting room, holding a tea towel in one hand and a large kitchen knife in the other. He appeared calm, almost too calm but there was a psychotic glint in his eye which terrified me.

'How, did you get in?' I stuttered. My brain felt frozen, as though it was processing everything at a very slow pace. What did he mean by cooking us dinner?

'Well the front door obviously. I've been watching where your friend Laura keeps her spare key. Not very inventive really is it? Under the door-mat?' He looked very pleased with himself. He knew Laura's name I thought in alarm. Was she okay.

'Laura. Is she okay?' I whimpered.

'She's fine,' he said sounding annoyed that I had asked about her.

'*Why* are you here Shane?' I asked quietly, acutely aware of the knife in his right hand.

'You kept ignoring my roses Kate and then I couldn't get through to you in the office.' He said this as though breaking into my house was obviously the next step. I willed my brain to start processing what was happening more quickly. I felt as though It was engulfed in a fog.

'I think you should go Shane,' I said trying to reassert myself.

'Don't be silly Kate,' he said with a calmness that completely unnerved me. 'I've cooked us a lovely dinner. Now we're just going to talk like friends.' He waved the knife around in the air as he spoke. My eyes were fixated on it as it glinted in the light.

'Why don't you put down the knife then Shane? There's no need for that among friends.'

'Now Kate I don't know yet if I can trust you so I'm going to keep the knife. Take out your mobile phone and put it on the table Kate. It wouldn't do for you to try and contact someone now would it and ruin our cosy evening together. I've been planning it for a *very* long time,' he said with a glint in his eye. He seemed lost in thought. 'All the time I was in Thameside I was thinking of you and planning how we could be together. My cell-mate thought I was crazy but here we are,' he said almost manically. His eyes had a crazed look in them. I was terrified.

'Your phone Kate,' he snapped, waving the hand which held the knife towards the table.

With a shaky hand I placed it on the table.

'Come Kate. You can help me by bringing the plates I've prepared from the kitchen into the table here. My hands are somewhat occupied,' he said waving the knife in the air once more.

I felt rooted to the spot and was still trying to get my head around the fact that Shane Reid was standing in my house waving a knife at me. Waving *my* knife.

263

'Kate,' he said with an edge to his voice. 'The plates.' He nodded in the direction of the kitchen. Maybe if I just played along and pretended that we were friends, we could have a dinner and he would leave. As much as I wanted this to be the case I knew that he had more sinister ideas for our evening. I walked past him to go into the kitchen and the stench of body odour from him made me want to retch. He looked like he hadn't shaved in quite a while and was sporting a grisly looking grey and ginger beard. His glasses had a crack in the right lens and there was black dirt under his finger nails.

In the kitchen it looked like he had heated up two microwave meals and put them onto plates.

'They're from M&S,' he said sounding almost proud. 'I know you like their food. I remember you ate sandwiches from there during my last trial.'

I doubted I would ever look at M&S food in the same light. A terrible thought crossed through my mind. What if I didn't make it out of here alive tonight? This meal with Shane could literally be my last supper.

'Pick them up,' he ordered. I walked slowly to the counter and as I picked them up Shane moved to stand behind me. I could feel his hot breath on my neck as he inhaled and exhaled deeply. He pressed the knife against the small of my back and placed his left hand on my bare neck and massaged it with his thumb. I closed my eyes shut willing him to stop.

'No, not now. Let's eat first,' Shane said almost to himself.

'Bring them to the sitting room,' he barked.

'Now you can have the choice of chilli con carne or Thai chicken,' he said as I put the plates on the table in the sitting room.

'Sit,' he ordered.

Complying I sat down in front of the Thai Chicken

plate. Any hunger I had felt earlier was now gone. I couldn't imagine eating the food which was congealing on the plate before me. I glanced over at his face, trying to discern what his intentions were. The knife was probably a pretty grim indication of what he might be planning.

'Eat Kate,' he said gesturing at my plate with his knife, his face forming into a scowl.

Tentatively I picked up the fork which was lying on the side of the plate. I immediately dropped it, when the door bell rang out shrilly. I was so tense that the everyday noise I was so familiar with had scared the life out of me. My heart was beating very fast.

'Who's that?' Shane demanded, looking uneasy. This hadn't been part of his plan. 'Who are you expecting?' he asked skittishly.

My Indian takeaway.

'Em, I'm not sure,' I stuttered, trying to sound believable.

'Stand,' he ordered. 'Walk to the window.'

Slowly I followed his directions. I was trying to give myself some time to figure out what to do.

'Faster,' he snapped.

At the window, he peered out through the curtains he must have pulled closed earlier.

'Did you order a takeaway Kate?' he said angrily. 'Why did you lie to me? You said you didn't know who was at the door?' His face was twisted with fury.

I stayed silent, unsure of what to say.

'Have you paid for it already?'

I nodded.

He pointed the knife at me. 'Walk to the door, take the food and close the door again.'

I had no choice but to follow his instructions. Silently I walked to the door and opened it just wide enough to be able to get my food through. The delivery man had his motor cycle helmet on and handed me the brown bag containing the food. I wanted to yell out or scream that a crazy man was in my house but Shane stood behind me and I was keenly aware of the knife pressed against the small of my back. Shutting the door, I felt as though I was closing the door on my only chance of escape.

'Now, back to our dinner,' he said pushing me roughly in the direction of the sitting room. He took the food bag from me and dropped it on the floor.

'Let's sit and enjoy our dinner,' he said smiling dangerously and pushing me into my chair. Sitting beside me he gripped the knife firmly in his left hand. He picked up a fork with his right hand and started shovelling the food into his mouth. He gestured for me to do the same.

Gingerly I put some cold rubbery chicken in my mouth and began to chew slowly. I had only taken a few bites when Shane had finished his plate. Have some lemonade he said pointing at my glass. It will help it go down easier. Picking up the glass I gulped back some of the warm liquid.

'Eat some more.'

I felt like a naughty child at a dinner table being ordered to eat their greens by an aggravated parent. I managed a few more forkfuls and drained the lemonade glass which seemed to satisfy him. I wondered what he had in store for me now. The lack of sleep last night must be catching up on me I thought, as the room was beginning to look a little foggy.

'Let's sit and watch some TV.' Shane ordered.

Hazily I stood and walked towards the couch. Shane sat beside me, uncomfortably close. I could feel the warmth of his body and smell the odour from him. I felt repulsed. He pointed the remote at the TV.

'I thought we could watch a romantic movie,' he

stated, as he flicked on Sleepless in Seattle. He sighed, in what sounded like contentment. I tried to unfog my mind and form a plan of action but it was getting harder and harder to concentrate.

'Isn't this nice? Shane asked placing his hand on my knee. I pulled it away.

'Don't be like that Kate,' he growled pointing the knife at me. Once again he placed his hand on my knee. I resisted my natural instinct to pull my leg away again. I didn't know what he would do with the knife if I did. The music for the start of the movie began. I looked at Shane out of the corner of my eye. He still had a strong grip on the handle of the knife. As the movie started I tried to work out how I could get out of here. My brain refused to cooperate. It felt hazy and I was fighting the urge to fall asleep. I stared numbly at the screen. I could hear Shane make some comment about Tom Hanks. He began to slide his hand up my leg. Think Kate, I urged myself.

I thought I heard Shane mumble something. I looked at him. I seemed to be viewing everything in slow motion.

'That's it Kate, just give into it,' I thought I heard him say. I felt confused. What was he talking about? Give into what? I struggled to remain focused but was finding it increasingly difficult. What was wrong with me?

Shane's hands moved to the band of my leggings and he pulled at them while pushing me back on the couch. I struggled weakly against his frame as he held me down. I felt feeble and tried to summon the strength to push him away as he stood over me, opening the buttons on his jeans. I knew what was about to happen but my body didn't seem to be able to fight the way I wanted it to.

The movie played on in the background and I was

fighting sleep. My eyes started shutting and the effort to keep them open was too difficult.

He pulled my leggings around my ankles and pushed up my jumper. I could hear him moaning and I shakily tried to push him back. His bulk was suddenly on top of me and his hand was rubbing furiously between my legs and his face was on my breasts. I was petrified but it felt as though I was watching the scene from afar and that I was powerless to do anything about it. I squirmed and tried to shout but the haze was getting stronger. It engulfed me and I was powerless to do anything but surrender to it.

CHAPTER FORTY

I felt groggy and my mouth was dry like I had been walking for many hours in the heat without water. I could hear a strange hum. I tried to focus. I blinked. There was a man sitting in a chair in the corner of the room.

'Shane?' I whispered, feeling a sense of panic rise up in me.

'Kate! You're awake.' The body rose and came towards me. I felt confused. It sounded like my dad.

'Dad?' I croaked.

'Darling, your okay now,' I heard my mother's voice from the other side of the bed.

A woman in white entered the room and took a clipboard from the end of my bed and started checking the readings on the machines beside my bed.

'You're in hospital darling. You've had a nasty fright but you'll be okay now,' my mum said in a soothing voice.

My father held a glass of water with a straw to my lips and I gratefully took a sip. I felt confused. How had I come to be in hospital? I shuddered as my last memory before I passed out came back to me. What had Shane done to me?

'Shane?' I questioned, fearfully.

'He's been arrested Kate,' my mother said. 'You won't need to worry about him anymore.'

'What happened? He made me eat some food and watch a movie. Then I think I fell asleep or passed out. I don't know how I did because I was so scared but maybe it was because I was so tired. I was so stupid.. '
I trailed off. My mother and father exchanged a look. My father gave my mother a slight nod as though allowing her to tell me what had happened.

'Hush, Kate, don't talk like that. None of this is your fault. He drugged you. The police have done tests on the food and drink he made you have and there was rohypnol found in the drink. I don't even want to think of what could have happened if that nice boy Alex hadn't arrived.' My father put his hand on my mother's shoulder, trying to comfort her. I could see that she was fighting off tears.

'Alex?' I asked in surprise. 'Alex arrived?'

'Yes, he saved you from, I don't even want to think of what could have happened to you,' Mum said.

'What did Shane do to me?' I asked, needing to know but almost dreading the answer.

'Oh Kate,' my mother sighed. 'The police think that he was going to rape you. But he didn't,' she hurriedly added. 'As I said, it's lucky that Alex turned up.'

'But he was preparing for a trial,' I said weakly. 'What was he doing at my house?'

'Apparently he wanted to surprise you,' my dad said with a smile. When he arrived he could tell that someone was inside because of the TV noise and the lights were on but no-one was answering the doorbell. He said for some reason he felt suspicious and managed to get in through the back door. He saw you passed out on the couch with that man on top of you.'

'Alex says that he pushed him off you and restrained him before calling the police and an ambulance. He's here now sweetie if you want to see him. They were only allowing family members in here but it shouldn't be a problem now that you are awake,' my mum added. She glanced at the nurse who nodded her head in consent.

I couldn't believe it. I literally had a knight in shining armour. My dad left the room to get Alex and my mum stroked my head which felt so soothing.

Moments later Alex followed my father through the

door and into my room. His eyes looked anxious and concerned.

'Right, well, we'll give you two some time to yourselves. We'll go and get a coffee Kate.'

'Thanks Dad,' I said gratefully.

As they left the room, Alex came nearer to the bed. I felt suddenly conscious of my hospital gown and wished I had asked mum to have a peek at her compact before he had come into the room.

'Alex, Mum and Dad told me what you did. I feel so grateful. Thank you so much,' I said looking at his warm eyes.

He took my hand and held it in his. He didn't try and say something stupid such as 'it was nothing.' We both knew that he had saved me from a horrible ordeal. He just nodded and continued to hold my hand. The hours passed by, nurses and doctors changed shifts but Alex was a constant. That night as I drifted into a fitful sleep he held my hand while I wondered if I would ever feel normal and unafraid again.